T0319058

Cambridge Elements ≡

Elements in Critical Heritage Studies
edited by
Kristian Kristiansen, *University of Gothenburg*
Michael Rowlands, *UCL*
Francis Nyamnjoh, *University of Cape Town*
Astrid Swenson, *Bath University*
Shu-Li Wang, *Academia Sinica*
Ola Wetterberg, *University of Gothenburg*

NATIVE AMERICANS IN BRITISH MUSEUMS

Living Histories

Jack Davy
University of East Anglia

CAMBRIDGE
UNIVERSITY PRESS

CAMBRIDGE
UNIVERSITY PRESS

University Printing House, Cambridge CB2 8BS, United Kingdom

One Liberty Plaza, 20th Floor, New York, NY 10006, USA

477 Williamstown Road, Port Melbourne, VIC 3207, Australia

314–321, 3rd Floor, Plot 3, Splendor Forum, Jasola District Centre,
New Delhi – 110025, India

103 Penang Road, #05–06/07, Visioncrest Commercial, Singapore 238467

Cambridge University Press is part of the University of Cambridge.

It furthers the University's mission by disseminating knowledge in the pursuit of
education, learning, and research at the highest international levels of excellence.

www.cambridge.org
Information on this title: www.cambridge.org/9781108829434
DOI: 10.1017/9781108909914

First published 2021

A catalogue record for this publication is available from the British Library.

ISBN 978-1-108-82943-4 Paperback
ISSN 2632-7074 (online)
ISSN 2632-7066 (print)

Native Americans in British Museums

Living Histories

Elements in Critical Heritage Studies

DOI: 10.1017/9781108909914
First published online: June 2021

Jack Davy
University of East Anglia
Author for correspondence: Jack Davy, j.davy@uea.ac.uk

Abstract: The accumulated collections of Native American material culture in museums in Britain are vast and of critical cultural importance. Drawing on interviews with Indigenous American visitors to UK museum displays and collections between 2017 and 2019, this Element highlights the most significant inadequacies of contemporary engagement with Native American visitors and communities, identifying fundamental problems rooted in the ethos of collection management and display. It then explores why two critical crises, one of representation and one of expertise, are together exacerbating these problems, and the damage to relationships and reputation which can result when these crises collide with Indigenous demands for greater agency in museum processes. The final section applies these lessons directly, developing an adaptable policy document to assist museum staff in effectively and respectfully managing their relationships with Indigenous communities and collections.

Keywords: museums, indigenous, heritage, Native American, policy

ISBNs: 9781108829434 (PB), 9781108909914 (OC)
ISSNs: 2632-7074 (online), 2632-7066 (print)

Contents

1 Introduction

In the ashes of the British fire that burned his cousins to the ground, what did Uncas see?

– Madeline Sayet, Mohegan, 2019i

On 17 June 2019, Mohegan playwright, actor and theatrical director Madeline Sayet gave a performance as part of the biennial Origins Festival at the Globe Theatre in London. Sayet was the first Native American playwright to stage a play at the theatre, and in the intimate mock-Tudor surroundings of the Sam Wanamaker Playhouse, she performed a self-penned, one-woman, one-act play named *Where We Belong*. Everything about the performance was designed to conspicuously situate Sayet as a Native woman operating within this quintessentially British space; her costume for example, was designed for the show by Cherokee-Navajo designer Asa Benally.

Sayet is a Shakespearean performer and director of considerable experience, who had come to England to study for a PhD in Shakespearean theatre. In Britain however she grappled with the complexities of being an Indigenous woman and Shakespeare scholar in a country which, it seems, finds it impossible to accept the combination of these two parts of her identity. She found herself continually coerced to study 'the primitive', 'the Native' or 'Caliban', forcing upon her a performative Indigeneity at odds with her intention, experience and knowledge of the subject. Lonely, and in search of solace and common experience, Sayet was driven to find traces of Native American presence in Britain, such as at the recently installed grave-marker of her Mohegan ancestor Mahomet Weyonomon at Southwark Cathedral.[1] It is in this vein that the play recounts a visit she made to the North American Gallery at the British Museum, where she was given a tour by an academic.

In the play, this experience is dramatically recreated: the academic is disdainful, sneering at the dead migratory birds on the glass roof of the Great Court and dismissive of repatriation claims from Indigenous Australians. In the gallery itself, Sayet stands in shock, 'looking at a mash of mislabelled indigenous objects, like varying nations crowded into a rail car – a continent facing genocide over hundreds and hundreds of years – wide spanses of geography thrown together in cases without specific acknowledgement' (Sayet, 2019:30).

---

[1] Mahomet Weyonomon was a sachem of the Mohegan people who travelled to London in 1735 to appeal to King George II against the seizure of Mohegan lands in Connecticut by English settlers. The appeal was referred to the Lords Commissioners, but Weyonomon died from smallpox before a decision was reached. He was buried in the grounds of Southwark Cathedral in an unmarked grave. In 2006, a memorial made of Connecticut granite was erected in the churchyard to commemorate Weyonomon, unveiled by Queen Elizabeth II and Mohegan tribal chairman Bruce Two Dogs Bozsmun.

On the question of human remains, of ancestors taken and repackaged as curiosities for European audiences, the academic is entirely transactional; 'No' he says, 'if we start giving back human remains, well they don't know where that would lead. They might have to give other things back.' Ultimately Sayet can only note with regret that she is 'sorry I have nothing to offer the spirits crowding the building, mashed up against friends, enemies, and strangers who don't understand them. I am scared to close my eyes and listen to the howling and pain around me.' Finally, she recounts 'I wander away into an exhibit on clocks and stare at it for a while – to cleanse my body of all the stolen stories, and objects of violence in this place. I want to go home' (Sayet, 2019:33). Far from finding solace in the museum, Sayet found pain.

The play moves on, Sayet telling of ending her PhD study early and returning home, where instead of criticism for not completing her course she finds acceptance and celebration at her travels and experiences in the footsteps of Mahomet Weyonomon. It was a powerful performance, which directly addressed the devastating legacies of colonialism among the Native peoples of the East Coast of North America. Throughout, she engages specifically with the chronic inability of British institutions, particularly those of education and knowledge, to meaningfully engage in a systematic way with those legacies – the academic at the British Museum for example is entirely insensitive to the pain his tour has caused, finishing the meeting with a ghost story, to which Sayet simply replies, 'You don't say . . .'

The importance of this kind of intervention into the British theatrical scene, the precedent it sets and the critical nature of the issues it addresses are at the heart of addressing decolonisation, and its meaning and reality, in the UK heritage and arts sectors. I saw this performance live, seated in the front row, so close that Sayet was within touching distance. Every emotion and experience on that stage was laid bare before my eyes, and this is important to note here because the performance was in some small way part of me and I was a small part of it, because I was the academic who gave her the tour of the British Museum.[2]

The tour was part of a months-long series of Skype and email conversations, including on-the-record interviews about her experience living in the UK, and I had intended the tour not to be a horror show of the violence of historic and

---

[2] Sayet has been effusive in making it clear that the academic who appears in her play is not meant to be me personally. Two months before the performance she wrote to me 'just FYI the section based on our conversation at the British Museum is not actually a reflection on you. It is not you – it is just the info and context of that conversation as is useful to further the storytelling of the questions of the piece' (Sayet, pers. com. 2019). After the performance she approached me directly to reassure me that the 'academic' of the piece was a stand-in for the neglect and disinterest, the disrespect, she felt from British institutions towards her and her people.

contemporary museum practice, but a discussion between peers of the acknowledged inadequacies of museum policy and display. During the conversation I made extensive efforts to provide content warnings about the subjects at hand, and to express my own frustrations with the failings of the institution. My excuses made, however, I must acknowledge that the words she quoted, though selectively, were mine, and that I clearly failed in my attempts to be sensitive to the impact my tour was having, and furthermore that despite years working with Indigenous communities and visitors, I had still not properly understood the degree to which the environment of the British Museum could be so directly and immediately traumatic for Sayet.

The stark reality of the trauma I had triggered for Sayet within an institution for which I worked for nearly a decade in a gallery which I helped to design, added an impetus to this research project. My intent to be supportive inadvertently became harmful through a lack of foresight and empathy, and gave a personal and powerful demonstration of the reasons why affecting and enabling a sector-wide and enduring shift in attitudes and approaches to Indigenous engagement encompassing displays, collections, visitors and relationships is so imperative. Sayet's account is particularly traumatic, and is not perhaps reflective of all Indigenous encounters in the museum spaces. Many, including some of the interviewees in this project, have positive, or at least productive, engagements with museums in Britain, in some cases lasting years.

Yet even for those less affected, the situation remains unacceptable; Professor Chris Andersen, (Michif), Dean of Indigenous Studies at the University of Alberta, acknowledged, for example, that while for him these experiences were less harmful than they were for Sayet, they were still accompanied by a feeling of 'irritation and annoyance' at stepping into a space so unrepresentative of his priorities in the display and study of material culture (Andersen, pers. com.2020).

These interactions are never easy; in the introduction to her book *Museums, Heritage and Indigenous Voice: Decolonizing Engagement,* Bryony Onciul writes that, 'While honourable in its intentions, the increasingly ubiquitous practice of community engagement in museums has often been under-analysed, and its difficulties and complexities understated' (2015:1). The first section in this Element, which documents the results of interviews with Native American visitors to museums in the UK, demonstrates that good intentions on the part of curators are not enough, they must be backed by actions which make a real positive impact. And these actions are becoming more urgent: there is an increasingly vocal movement in the UK towards a model of Indigenous representation in the museum sector, one which is respectful of Indigenous protocol and authority. Change is coming – it is only the terms which must be negotiated, as well as the circumstances under which they are imposed. Art historian Alice Procter has noted to this point that 'it feels as if we are in a moment, now, that might be a turning point. There is more public conversation around repatriation and restitution that has been building up for a while, and it seems as if it is part of a bigger, international anxiety around national identity and nationalism' (Procter, 2020:11).

This forms part of a broader movement, expanded in detail in Section 2 and termed in this work the representation crisis. This crisis is not an academic exercise or a theoretical position, it is a direct and actively harmful theatre of colonial and post-colonial exchange in which power imbalances exacerbate and amplify past harm into present and future harm. This crisis is worsened by a second movement, termed here the expertise crisis, in which expertise with Indigenous collections is being stripped from the heritage sector by unplanned structural changes.

The research which this Element compiles and analyses was developed within the Arts and Humanities Research Council–funded project *Beyond the Spectacle*, hosted by the Universities of Kent and East Anglia. This project has sought to explore the complicated histories of Native American travellers to Britain, reaching back to the earliest visitors in the sixteenth century and continuing up to the present day. In my role in this project as a Research Associate, I took an interest in the subject of museum displays of Native American material culture, and to what extent the displays were representative or meaningful to Native Americans living in or visiting Britain. The research was conducted with Native American visitors to museums in Britain during the period of this project 2017–20 willing to collaborate with the project, and in consequence most interviewees are focused on case studies in museums in south-eastern England.[3]

1.2 Project Goals

What Sayet's play makes clear is that there are huge problems of representation in museums in Britain, which are caught in the midst of the two crises. Her play,

---

[3] This publication is thus a product of *Beyond the Spectacle,* an Arts & Humanities Research Council–funded research project which examines the histories of Native North American travellers to Britain. For the purposes of this project and this Element, the terms Native North American, Native American and Indigenous indicate a person descended from the inhabitants of the continent pre European colonisation. While we have been alert to the risk of imposters, the project has not attempted to police who does and does not have the right to this identification. Since this funding was specifically entailed towards an examination of Native American histories in Britain the recommendations which follow reflect that research focus. This publication is however intended to be written in such a way that its recommendations can, with adaptation, be deployed to other collections and peoples from other continents.

and the interviews with other Native visitors which follow, make it clear that museums and museum staff must come to a better accommodation with Indigenous stakeholders, and that until they do so the heritage sector is not effectively decolonising at all, but rather all-too-often inadvertently entrenching colonialism through inaction, indifference or ignorance. This Element has two clear goals. The first is to present in context a body of evidence from Native visitors about the ways in which the UK museum sector is currently inadequately responding to Indigenous demands for better agency in museum spaces – the representation crisis – during one of the toughest funding environments museums have faced since their establishment – the expertise crisis. It also tries to offer hope by identifying and articulating solutions to this problem as identified by Native partners and interviewees.

The second goal, developed in Section 3 from the preceding discussions, is to present a simple policy road map which should help mitigate the most significant and problematic failings, those caused by a lack of training or expertise in the sector. This policy document is intended to be an adaptable and amendable guide for staff working with Indigenous collections nationwide, intended to be formally accepted as aspirational policy and integrated into basic collections management protocols moving forward. The policy is not, though, solely tailored to accommodate those small numbers of Indigenous visitors like Sayet who pass through museum spaces and engage with collections – it encourages museum staff to work directly with Indigenous communities on developing their displays, managing their collections and providing interpretation for non-Indigenous visitors.

Public education on Native American history in Britain is tiny – most visitors will know little more than they have haphazardly collected from films and television. Museums which display Indigenous American material therefore have an opportunity to educate visitors beyond these stereotypes and illustrate not only the diverse, often-tragic and always-complex histories of Native communities, but also their vibrant and joyful present; Onciul for example, noted that 'Heritage sites and museums are important points of entry for Indigenous' peoples' voices into mainstream society because they have the ability to validate identities, histories, culture and societies' (2015:8). The next section will present a thematic road map for this type of education, with a practical policy developed further in Section 3.

As with all such studies, it is no more than a snapshot in space and time, reflective of a sector undergoing deep and often uncontrolled change in a world that is likewise shifting rapidly. There are many museums in Britain which already practice some or all of the recommendations here, and inevitably some of these recommendations will be seen as obsolete in just a few years' time. It is my hope though that this short survey will join the growing body of work which is insisting that museums in Britain can and should do things in ways which better reflect the complexity of Indigenous experiences and histories. In this, it does not make academic debate the goal, but seeks to generate and provide working museum staff with the tools to make meaningful, if small, differences in their practices to provide at least some of those tools to begin to mitigate the errors of the past and help to promote healing, understand problematic history and mitigate the potential for harm

2 Native American Visitors to Museums in the UK

Mvskoke scholar Taylor Norman noted in her 2019 study of UK museum techniques and practices towards Native American collections that without an accommodation for the harm of the past, the damage Sayet illustrates can become widespread, and she rightly calls for better Indigenous representation in the museum space as a pre-requisite for addressing this problem:

> Without *state* acknowledgement of wrongdoing via harmful policies, the onus of presenting our side of the story lies with Indigenous people, namely our work to counteract centuries of lies spun to effectively enable harm. When a museum presents our cultures in a way that affirms these lies, untruths, or even partial truths, they facilitate harmful thinking which can have direct consequence in Native lives. (Norman, 2019i:15)

This acknowledgement gives cause for hope despite the crises museums face, because just as the museum is not a neutral environment, effective engagement is not a neutral or balancing act, but a positive one. There are currently dozens of decolonisation projects ongoing in UK museums and heritage organisations, and the last decades have yielded a portfolio of hundreds more. Museums and museum staff have worked and continue to work productively with Indigenous partners across the country; most recently the curators of the Arctic Exhibition at the British Museum, who collaborated with a number of Inuit partners, including the Embassy of Imagination at Cape Dorset, Nunavut (Cooper, 2020). This increased prevalence of collaborative projects has been noticed by Indigenous heritage activists, and each small project incrementally advances the broad case in small, specific ways, and if ethically managed, each can gradually start to mitigate harm and improve public education.

One such example took place in 2018, when the Horniman Museum opened its new World Galleries, replacing a twenty-year-old display of African art with a far broader permanent exhibition of objects from all over the world. I was part of the curatorial team working on this project, and part of the display we developed was an installation which was known, in the planning phase, as the

'Totem interactive'. The curators invited Steve Smith, a Kwakwaka'wakw artist from the Northwest Coast region of North America, to produce three mask-faces of traditional figures from Kwakwaka'wakw oral history. These were then mounted on cedar pillars with buttons which, when pushed, caused stories from these oral histories to be played on a speaker.

Aimed at the Horniman's predominately juvenile audience, these installations allow visitors to learn about Kwakwaka'wakw stories in unconventional ways. They can both touch an object – gain a sense of the texture and smell of cedar wood and thus give the display more context than mere visual presentation can allow – as well as hear a story which brings the figures on display to life. They are not static depictions solely for the aesthetic enjoyment of non-Indigenous visitors, but mask-faces collaboratively designed to educate, entertain and speak simultaneously to British audiences, Indigenous communities and beings invisible. By making connections between the oral histories of dynamic living communities and their historic material culture, showing these communities as still thriving, this project sought to educate in a way that minimises the risks of past harms turning into future harm.

These stories were formally told to the Horniman Museum by Sierra Tasi Baker, a Kwakwaka'wakw storyteller, artist and activist, who first obtained permission from the relevant family and tribal authorities to record and repeat the inherited stories for a British audience. The import of this collaboration was not lost on the participants, both within the museum and from the Native community. Tasi Baker later emphasised this in an interview for this Element:

> This [interactive storytelling exhibit] is a really good precedent, for how I think museums should be showcasing our culture. The entire process itself was really respectful of protocol … I really appreciate how that was done, very nuanced, and very well understood … I think it's a better way of showing our culture than a mask behind glass, and it shows that our culture is living, that it is a living culture.
>
> I think the more that researchers start shifting towards realising that they're helping to change the narrative, and shift the narrative, and understanding that they are agents of reconciliation I think that researchers will realise that their work opens up quite a bit more. The more they realise that research is a form of healing. I think that would be really amazing if academics could figure that one out. (Tasi Baker, 2018)

The solution that Tasi Baker suggests therefore is at once simple and complex. It amounts to no more than listening to people for whom these issues are most important and acting on their recommendations, while at the same time it demands adoption of new and holistic methods of conversation and engagement to achieve results beyond simple fixes to presentational issues, in essence an inversion of how such displays are designed, developed and installed. If research is to be a form of healing, then it requires active participation from multiple partners and crucially, the peoples for whom the healing is most necessary. Properly managed, this idea is one which not only avoids future distress, but also begins to mitigate some of the pain of the past. It is this in particular to which Tasi Baker was referring; that by coming together and researching together rather than operating separately or antagonistically, museums and Indigenous communities can promote healing through cross-cultural education, opportunity, exploration and trust-building.

Jisgang Nika Collison, Curator of the Haida Gwaii Museum, has described this process as one of facilitation:

> When people ask me what I'm an expert in, I say, 'knowing where to go.' As in, where the knowledge is. A lot of my work is facilitation. Facilitating the knowledge and stories of incredible, complex people, places, and histories. I didn't like the word 'curator' when I started out. For me the word was quite elitist, individualistic, and prohibitive to real audience engagement. But then I took a class taught by Carol Mayer who used the word 'facilitation' when talking about curation. That changed my mind about what a curator is, can be, or should be. (Collison & Levell, 2018)

Drawing on the theories employed in the work of truth and reconciliation commissions, Norman has branded this curatorial work collectively as 'truth-telling'. She is clear that there can be no place for stereotypes or ignorance in displays which perpetuate the kind of harm Sayet encountered, and that ultimately there is a widespread social good in counteracting them: 'Truth-telling about Native American issues is about more than appeasing source communities, it must hold prominence if museological institutions intend to be honest in their engagement with current social politics' (Norman, 2019i:15–17).

Research becoming a form of healing thus requires truth-telling. This approach is essential in understanding how museums can provide institutional platforms not as pseudo-neutral educational environments, but as active agents of decolonisation, mitigating harm and acknowledging truths, no matter how uncomfortable for a domestic British audience. In part, harm perpetuates because, as Norman and Sayet suggest, this truthful collaborative approach is already hoped for by some Native visitors to UK museums, and its absence can deepen the discomfort they encounter.[4] Research for this Element has demonstrated again and again that many Indigenous North American people view (or expect to view) museum spaces as Indigenous environments in which they can

---

[4] Taylor Norman has clarified that the main issue here is difference in museums between 'how [Indigenous people] are presented and how they present themselves. The dissonance is entirely on the institutions' side' (pers. com.).

find the solace Sayet sought, and that when they are unable to experience museums in the UK in this way, an emotional response, whether mild irritation or emotional harm, is triggered and exacerbated, not mitigated. As with the tour I gave to Madeline Sayet, encounters which to British museum staff seem routine and benign can, in the context of Native peoples encountering legacies of colonial harm in gallery spaces, become distressing. Good intentions are not enough, if the impacts are harmful.

An example of this was discussed at interview with Danielle Baca, a student of Ute, Apache and Pueblo descent, who explained that she had long been disassociated from her Indigenous heritage, a consequence of her Native family members 'dying too early and rejecting who they are' during the twentieth century. Baca noted that this history of grief and erasure had had a serious impact on her personal identity, that 'I've always been taught to not be comfortable with whom I am. I've always been taught that it leads to a lot of bad things.' Studying in London in 2018/19, she sought to research 'Native American identity and well-being', employing autoethnography – academic analysis of personal experience – in her engagement with UK museums, and in particular the British Museum. In effect, she was treating the museum space as a site of unstructured personal reconciliation, but in that environment she found that even seemingly innocuous encounters could become troubling:

> It sounds sinister, but to get what I want, what I need, in some contexts yes, [I have to hide who I am]. I go to the BM a lot to take photos of different objects in the Museum. I like to go and write. Usually once or twice a week I just go and sit in the Native American Collection and write my feelings out. It feels good, and I like to immerse myself in it that way. And I have been asked by staff . . . who I know worked there because of the way that they displayed their authority on their lanyard on with the badge, who just asked 'what are you doing here?'
>
> I felt like my behaviour looked [pause]. I was kind of on my knees to take a photo of something and then I was moving around and reading things and then I was sitting on the bench to write, and I think he was noticing those behaviours. And you sit in that moment and you have to make that decision in seconds, but I wasn't going to say 'I'm an Indigenous person with feelings, about this and that', so what I would say is, 'I'm a student'. I chose that brief, trivialised version of it, and they said 'OK' and walked away. (Baca, 2019)

Baca's story highlights an essential disconnect in engagement between Native visitors seeking a meaningful experiential encounter and British or tourist audiences in search of a learning or entertainment experience. I am certain that the staff member in this instance did not mean to cause offense or appear threatening; their inquiry was ostensibly good-natured and polite, and did not reflect wider policy or suspicion on the part of the institution, but it is clear that ignorance of how an Indigenous person might experience the gallery, coupled with a gentle but unmistakable exertion of non-Indigenous authority over an ostensibly Indigenous space triggered discomfort in Baca and prevented her from using the space in the way she had intended.

Even in this brief conversation, so seemingly innocuous to those not living with the enduring legacies of colonial oppression, Baca felt unwelcome, both personally and on a broader cultural level. Part of this discomfort comes from the realisation that her mode of engagement with the collections in ways that were meaningful to her as a person of Indigenous decent were unusual enough to attract official attention, precisely the thing her ancestors, who so assiduously practised self-erasure of their Indigenous heritage, would have feared.

Baca and Sayet both approached these museum spaces not as sources of information or entertainment as would a British or tourist visitor, but as memorial spaces in which the objects are inextricably entangled in cultural memory which by their very presence exacerbates the existing internalised trauma of being an Indigenous person in a so-called post-colonial period. Baca's journey was, for family reasons, a journey of self-discovery or rediscovery in which trauma was unexpectedly located over time, whereas for Sayet, by education and profession more closely associated and familiar with marginalised trauma, the impact was immediate and devastating. In both cases though the harm was real and substantial – a space that could have been one of compassion and connection became one of separation and erasure.

Part of the problem is that the living cultures Tasi Baker advocated are missing from displays, which can leave visitors with the impression that Native culture stopped developing at some point in the early twentieth century. Taylor Norman recounted visiting museums in London, searching for but not finding the contemporary material culture of her people and discussion of modern Indigenous life: 'I did feel largely erased with both the British Museum and Horniman's displays as a Black Mvskoke woman … My visits became more about observation than engagement with my tangible cultural heritage, despite the rich stores of Creek artefacts that exist in London currently' (Norman, 2019i:30). Narragansett student Kimonee Burke criticised the British Museum displays at interview, noting that 'for me it felt very sterile, and it always feels very wrong to see objects from home in such a foreign and unnatural environment. These are real parts of our culture and history and seeing them removed and put behind a glass case it always feels wrong personally … My tribe wasn't even listed as being in the region!' (Burke, 2019).

The issue these Indigenous women all describe is best engaged with on a theoretical level using Mary Louise Pratt's concept of the contact zone, an environment that occurs when there is a clash or collaboration between distinct cultures potentially struggling with 'asymmetrical relations of power' (Pratt, 1991:34). The term was first applied in a museum setting in relation to a visit to the Portland Museum of Art by a delegation from the Tlingit people in 1987 (Clifford, 1999 [1997]), and has subsequently led to a paradigmatic shift in the ways in which museums collaborate with Indigenous visitors, with institutions striving to better recognise Indigenous motivations in engaging with collections, and how relationships which exist between Indigenous visitors and their objects differ from the more common non-Indigenous visitors and those same objects.

Professor Elizabeth Edwards has summarised this movement, commending the collegiate approach it entails:

> Post-colonial cultural and identity politics and the recognition of the claims of the formerly colonised on those histories have become part of the air breathed in such museums in the last 20 years. They have not so much simply 'decolonised' their practices and collections, for such actions might strip out precisely the history that should be robustly addressed. Rather, they have worked to confront and explore their complex global histories, and engage with the needs, demands and desires that have arisen from these deeply troubled and appropriative historical relationships. (Edwards, 2018)

This has led to the establishment of various guidelines and policies for museums to follow in their engagements with Indigenous communities: good examples include those produced by the School of Advanced Research in Santa Fe and the Smithsonian Center for Folklife and Cultural Heritage (2019; n.d., respectively). Most institutions in North American now have some variant of these guides for their staff and for external partners. These however are tailored to the specifics of North American museums, and generally lack the specificity or practical advice needed for museums in the UK, which have quite different structures and histories.

Underpinning all of these efforts is the acknowledgement, noted by James Clifford, that for Indigenous visitors 'the collected objects are not primarily "art"', but rather 'aide-mémoires, occasions for the telling of stories and the singing of songs' (Clifford, 1999 [1997]:435–7). Nadia Clerici has recognised that during these encounters, the Native visitors typically 'try to make non-Indians understand their contemporary reality in historical perspective' (Clerici, 2002:3), but have found, in the words of Laura Peers, that 'consultation is often structured to provide outside support for the maintenance of institutional practices, and source community members are wary of contributing to museum-led consultation exercises which do not lead to change within museums or benefits to their people' (Peers & Brown, 2003:2). Norman has noted that it is not just the search for knowledge that is problematic in these exchanges, but the way museums root that knowledge in the material; 'when we continually place an emphasis on objects and their importance to museums, we contribute to the narrative that museums are unable to educate without them, subsequently constricting innovation in the sector' (Norman, 2019i:27).

One of the most important projects examining this phenomenon in Britain took place in 2009, when a large delegation from Haida Gwaii spent several weeks at the British Museum and the Pitt-Rivers Museum viewing collections as part of a visual repatriation project. During this experience 'the museum received a fraction of the information that the Haidas did, primarily that which the delegates felt was important for the museum to know about the identification or name or function of an object'. This was not therefore a case of the museum benefiting from Indigenous consultants whose primary task was to provide expertise and information for exhibitions or other museum purposes. For example, although 'the Haida expected to generate knowledge for themselves, knowledge that would be put into practice in various ways in their community when they went home', one of the most important goals of the visiting delegation was to negotiate the repatriation of human remains from the museums to Haida Gwaii (Krmpotich & Peers, 2013:35).

In this project, Indigenous ambitions were the driving force behind its conception and execution and the museums served as facilitators between the preserved collections and Native visitors rather than as equal partners sharing in the knowledge produced by the project at will. Instead it was left to the Indigenous visitors to decide how to interact with the objects (within the bounds of safety for participants and objects), what information to share with the museum, and how complete that information would be. Though this project yielded a large quantity of valuable data on Haida encounters with the museum space, its findings – and those of the many other decolonisation projects in UK museums before and since – are slow to find their way into the museum galleries: neither the British Museum nor the Pitt-Rivers have, for example, substantially redesigned their displays in the ensuing decade in response to this feedback, and opportunities to better educate were missed.

2.1 Changing Museum Ethos

Based on Sayet and Baca's accounts, it would be useful to think of their encounters through a comparison of museums of world cultures, such as the British Museum, and memorial museums which commemorate and acknowledge trauma explicitly. In her study of memorial museums, Amy Sodaro notes that their essential quality is that they 'serve as a space of healing and repair; in this they are a form of symbolic reparation that seeks to give acknowledgment to the victims and serve as a solemn space of mourning and remembrance in the effort to help heal and repair a community' (2018:162).

Kwakwaka'wakw artist Sonny Assu described at interview how the idea of museums as a space of memorial functions in relation to his own art practice, emphasising that museums are not just places for remembering past actions and the impact of colonialism, but also active sites of intergenerational supernatural exchange, echoing Sayet's recognition of the 'spirits crowding the building'. Describing an artwork he produced for an exhibition at the Sainsbury Centre for Visual Arts in Norwich, he noted:

> At the background there's these other half ovoid shapes that are mostly in black and grey with these really intense red eyes looking down. So for me these represent the ancestors. And those are the ancestors that are watching these foreground figures dance like the ancestors are watching. You know I think it's a quote by Audrey Hepburn, 'Dance as though no one is watching'? ... think about it in relationship to being an Indigenous person and reclaiming your identity and moving past that notion of shame and your cultural identity. Cause for a long time that was part of the process, was you had to feel shame, and being an Indigenous person and feeling shame and practicing your culture ... it's important to understand that our ancestors are watching us. And whether it's dancing or holding ourselves accountable for what we do, we need to act for those people who are watching over us. That they are not necessarily judging us but they're gonna be holding us account-able. (Assu, 2019)

Native museum professionals working in North America have long understood this function of the museum space as one of both healing and projection, a place for both remembrance and the transmission of positive Native histories. Sayet recounted at interview how the Native-run museums with which she was more familiar, like the Tantaquidgeon Museum in her home community, have a set-up which presents Native peoples as both living, vibrant and collaborative with non-Native society: 'I grew up in that museum, giving tours ... my family founded the museum in the 1920s with the idea that it's hard to hate somebody you know a lot about. And so the whole framework was like living Native people telling stories about living objects, right?' (Sayet, 2019ii:4) The Tantaquidgeon Museum is thus centred on the notion of research as healing – that by welcoming in and educating Native and non-Native audiences alike, reconciliation and healing are promoted within the very ethos of the institution. The advantage the Tantaquidgeon Museums has over museums in the UK on this approach is the ready availability of living Indigenous people able to engage with visitors and the collections. In Britain, where there is no Native American diaspora, other solutions must be found to facilitate this type of engagement, solutions which require a change in approach, and a change of ethos.

In discussing her positive experience at the Globe, where she was a key performer within the Origins Festival, Sayet described her surprise at walking into an ethos far less formal and restrictive than she had imagined. Staff there provided her with a lavender-scented rehearsal/nap space for the duration of her short residency, and supplied her with lemon, honey and ginger tea for her strained voice. She said of the space: 'It was very kind, and I think they actually cared about and appreciated and felt like this and wanted to do work like that, which meant so much about the future.' She went on to note:

> If I had shown up and they had been trepidacious ... it would have been a very hard thing to do. But that's not what happened. Instead I consistently got like 'We're so excited for you to be here!' Gestures of love, warmth and kindness, and generosity. And lots of hugs, you know, things that make us feel warm instead of things that make us feel cold. (Sayet, 2019ii)

It is this ethos – one of 'love, warmth and kindness' – seemingly nebulous from a professional curatorial viewpoint but to Indigenous visitors very real, that is too often missing in museums in the UK, and in its absence, the healing Tasi Baker describes is perhaps impossible, certainly less tangible. For Indigenous American visitors, the collections they visit are not abstractions or curiosities, but the tangible material evidence both for a cultural heritage left catastrophically damaged, of the genocide which caused the damage and, for Baca and many others, potentially the key to a more positive self-identity. In their absence from home communities and in their presence in museums these objects stand for a loss which there can be no compensation, but perhaps, though better treatment of people and collections there might be some healing, even celebration, and promotion of better education for British visitors.

As an example, in 2019, during the negotiations which resulted in the return of ancestral remains removed from gravesites by archaeologists in the early twentieth century and owned by the Bristol Museum, Tongva curator Desiree Martinez explained:

> As Native Americans, we are in a constant state of mourning knowing that our ancestors' graves have been disturbed and their remains and burial goods removed to sit on museum shelves, all over the world, to be 'studied' ... [T]oday we are joyful that we can bring our ancestors back to the US and rebury them in their homelands. (Postans, 2019)

Joy is not a word commonly used by Native visitors in relation to museums which house their collections: as illustrated in Baca and Sayet's narratives, trauma and grief can often play much more significant parts. Yet if a museum can provide an ethos in which collaboration and research can lead to healing, it may yet be able to provoke joy, an emotion which can fundamentally alter how the representation crisis plays out in the UK museum sector and how museums present Indigenous cultures to British audiences.

The research for this Element has highlighted four key themes, each raised in some form repeatedly at interview with Indigenous scholars and visitors, which I posit are the foundational building blocks of redesigning the museum ethos and gallery space to promote healing and potentially, joy, starting with recognition of nuance and complexity in Indigenous societies. These are not yet calls for hard action – practical policy advice on addressing these crises is presented in Section 4, informed and underpinned by these themes. Rather these are suggestions for the aspirational, ideological alterations to curatorial approaches necessary for collaborative healing to become the norm within museums, rather than exceptional and sporadic projects, and they are loosely defined as location, absence, complexity and living cultures.

2.2 Love, Warmth and Kindness

(1) Where Is the Display?

The first theme considers the ethics of physical displays, the moral underpinnings of how, by whom and for whom museum displays are designed, and to rethink how they might be more effectively employed. Gallery spaces showcasing Indigenous objects in the UK are almost never designed for Indigenous experience, but for European experiences, and all too often omit the reality of their origins, extracted from oppressed populations undergoing cultural genocide. A European space resembles a traditional art gallery space, in which objects are viewed at a distance behind glass, while a Native space is more communal, in which an institution is more about, as Chitimacha/Choctaw artist Sarah Sense noted at interview, 'taking care and creating a calm space to experience objects' (Sense, 2019)

This disconnected reality, inescapably imprinted in the very architectural formats of museums and galleries in the UK, is unavoidable and ever-present, but no longer an issue which can be safely ignored in gallery display and interpretation. Displays must now acknowledge the histories, specific and general, by which objects reached museums and appeared in displays, assemblages 'not made according to a deliberate plan to tell a specific story. Instead the objects came from explorers, missionaries and traders, then circulated in a secondary market that deprived them of any provenance information obtained by their initial collectors' (King, 2012:57).

These diverse and fragmentary trajectories of individual objects need to be explained clearly in the gallery spaces, a collective acknowledgement of the entangled histories of the objects within the great colonial web of trade, warfare and cultural assimilation of empire. Such an acknowledgement should for museums in Britain be as standard as land acknowledgements – paying respect to the ancestral inhabitants of the land on which you are standing – are now becoming in North American institutions; a recognition of the entangled and potentially harmful histories which bind the objects and institutions, they are an essential step if healing is to be meaningfully promoted. Jenny Marlowe, an activist of Ojibwe descent, has given this a lot of thought, and notes that museums present a really interesting opportunity for land acknowledgement:

> I think you really have to engage with the idea that museums by their very nature are archives, they are collections of the past. And so I think that what is really interesting for Native North American peoples specifically ... [is that] these are living cultures. We're still here, and the types of cultural objects and cultural histories that are likely to be collected in museums, are living histories. These are things that are still very, very important to Native cultures. So I don't know, you might have a headdress displayed, or any piece of regalia really, but something that is still currently very sacred and very active part of a living culture. This is not to say that the culture is mired in the past, but that there are a lot of cultural customs that still are important and relevant today, and I think there is a way to acknowledge that that is not so much a land acknowledgment as a cultural acknowledgment. (Marlowe, 2020)

Museums must begin by recognising that these spaces are always designed and approached explicitly as galleries of colonially assembled objects – places to look at foreign things only, but also that this category of space can mean different things to different audiences. Linda Coombes of the Aquinnah Wampanoag, for example, on seeing a wampum belt in the British Museum expressed that 'just to view it was for me, you know, a great honour. Knowing what these belts mean to the people that made them, and what they were used for' (Coombes, 2019).

Art historian Alice Procter has identified this reality for art and communities which operate outside the scientific paradigm of museum origins, noting that

> When religious art moves into a museum space the assumption is generally that it will no longer be an object of devotion. Sometimes, particularly with objects of non-European origin which are now in European museums, communities break that assumption in order to revere the sacred objects of their

culture ... Museums tend to tolerate this, though they may not endorse it. (Procter, 2020:68)

In such cases, by thinking differently about how the space is designed and occupied, the gallery could become a space where the collaborative research so necessary for healing might take place.

This can only be achieved through direct collaboration. British curators, no matter how knowledgeable, experienced or well-meaning, cannot live the experience of visiting a museum collection bound with the weight, meaning or risk of trauma Sayet describes. It is imperative therefore that museums take the steps necessary to ensure that people who can experience these emotions are properly consulted at every stage of a proposed gallery development or major project.

Expanding on this emotional significance, Taylor Norman notes that what museums think of objects and what Indigenous communities think of objects are often markedly different, but that there is a third partner in this exchange whose voices are rarely directly considered – the objects themselves. She writes that 'recognizing that not all objects are simply objects – some are ancestors, some need to breathe, some need to be fed, and some are not meant to be preserved – it is crucial that Indigenous curation practices, many of which predate Western Museums, be acknowledged. (Norman, 2019i:23)

The changes that are essential to facilitate these requirements need not be dramatic in the first instance – changes can be as simple as providing spaces of reflection and learning within the gallery, or minor alteration to storage facilities. A few benches and reference books for example, particularly texts written by Native scholars that emphasise Indigenous ways of encountering and engaging with material culture. Particularly if these spaces are sited at points of the greatest cultural impact and speak directly to the objects on display in that space, properly interpreted and displayed through collaborative practice. More significant changes though will be required over time as spaces are redesigned.

(2) What is missing?

As a second theme, leading on from the first and requiring more direct intervention, museums should think not only about what is there, but about what is missing. Taylor Norman discussed feeling excluded in gallery spaces which overgeneralised Native experience:

> You don't get to see the diversity of Native peoples. So somebody like me, who is Black and Native, you can't tell that we exist at all from looking at the objects or just the thumbnail pictures that you see. You can't see the diversity of Native America and you also can't see how all of the cultures have meshed

and intermingled and everything, so it's not just stark regions, right? Because nothing was just set. (Norman, 2019ii)

Her point is that Native people are not and never have been homogenous, or neatly organised within collective groupings which make for neat displays. This has long been understood as problematic in scholarship of Native histories; in 1999, anthropologist Aaron Glass warned of 'the dangers of eclipsing geographic and historical variation' in Native American scholarship (1999:191–3), and failing to acknowledge the vast diversity of identity and viewpoints within individual Native communities, let alone within pan-continental movements. Yet in museums these problematic oversimplifications have too often persisted.

The solution of course, as Sayet makes clear, is that 'if you want Native perspectives, let Native people talk about it' (Sayet, 2019ii:5), and one of the key points made in the interviews quoted here is to question where objects are actually located. Though the collections of Native American material in museums are large, compared with the lost material and the lost techniques, stories and histories they come from, they are tiny, and full of gaps. Linda Coombes came to Britain to look for wampum belts, but left disappointed; 'I was a little shocked that there wasn't more information. I thought there would be, but there wasn't. Some of them they weren't even sure what people they came from, what tribe, you know?' She went on, 'I thought that there was a ton of belts in the British Museum, but it doesn't seem like there are. I don't know ... Ideally it would be great if they could come home, but a lot of times there isn't even, as I was saying, the information as to even what people they come from.' (Coombes, 2019)

Kimonee Burke also commented on this aspect at the British Museum, noting that to a casual visitor the displays look unimpressive in contrast to the material the museum owns in its storage facilities.

> I feel like for me, focusing on the New England section as the one I was most interested in, they were missing a lot. I think they described it as some kind of Peoquot Empire, which is debatable ... but they were missing a bunch of tribes from Southern New England. I had an issue with how they had selected what they considered to be relevant groups from North America, considering there were like 600 tribes. It seemed like a weird selection and an oddly grouped selection to address their objects with little to no explanation of how they got them and little to no explanation of what they were. I think for me it was kind of confusing ... I don't really know how they curated the display, who chose the objects or how they wrote the blurbs. (Burke, 2019)

The combination of missing information and missing objects where objects were expected to be found is clearly a disconcerting experience – museums are supposed to be treasure houses of missing culture, resources for Native people to draw on in rebuilding lost histories. Curator Nika Collison of the Haida has posited that this was a deliberate process, that ancestors placed prohibited information in museums where future generations could rediscover it, a process she calls the 'string' which connects modern Haida with their ancestors (Collison, 2016). Haida artist Gwaii Edenshaw supports this idea, and he has noted that among his people there were artists who worked simply to preserve tradition and culture in the face of aggressive assimilation policies:

> There were other artists, in that time period and later, who weren't natural artists, but for whatever reason carried forwards that huge body of slate work that kind of has that naïve aspect to it when you consider the formality of the art ... I'm really grateful that they sort of kept that unbroken line of work from the height of our art to the new renaissance that we are in now.' (Davy, 2021)[5]

It is for this reason that it is vitally important that names of artists are included in interpretation, so that these kinds of links can be drawn. This is of course true of contemporary Indigenous artists; Sarah Sense noted at interview

> understanding of different types of art that come out of Native North America and the best ways to display them ... that carefulness would begin with labelling. I don't see why a living native artist in a British museum would not have their name on the label. I think that it's incredibly problematic and it's a disconnect. It disconnects community and individual from the institution. (Sense, 2019)

Museums therefore have, for some Native visitors, a specific responsibility to preserve collections for future generations of Indigenous peoples. This makes the absences in documentation, in collections and in voice all the more jarring, because museums never consciously sought to be representative storehouses of knowledge for colonised peoples – their modes of representation were and are tailored to the dominant colonisers, not the colonised, and thus have not traditionally valued or preserved information which does not meet the requirements of the former audience, at the expense of the latter.

Norman states that 'good-faith relations between museums and Indigenous people around the world rely on a willingness to tell our truths, to display out tangible heritage in a respectful manner, and to not contribute to our erasure' (Norman, 2019i:36), and as Sense concludes,

---

[5] This Element uses the term *artist* to refer to any person who makes or has made an object which has found its way to public display. It does not distinguish between those who intended their work to be displayed in a museum and those who did not, nor does it make any judgement on quality or whether that display is appropriate in context.

> I would say that when it comes to colonial histories between the UK and Native North America there's a lot of broken trust because of broken treaties. With that, things that were taken, removed and then people being displaced, there's loss. There's cultural loss. There's ceremonial loss. There's land loss. Medicinal loss. Family loss. Family ruptures. I think that recognition of what happened and that it was wrong, trying to reinforce some of the art and undo the colonial ways of running a museum could definitely contribute towards a more constructive healing process. (Sense, 2019)

Museums must acknowledge and confront this selective and partial accumulation of knowledge within their collections. They must acknowledge it to Indigenous visitors to mitigate the disappointment Coombes and others have described; they must acknowledge it to themselves if they are to improve curatorial practice; and they must acknowledge it to British audiences, so that they can fulfil their duties to educate and inform and thereby improve public engagement with the issues at stake. This will require honesty about missing or partial documentation and eccentric collecting practices, and acknowledgement of the inadequacies in attempting to present universal holistic displays covering disparate and often diffuse material cultures across vast temporal and geographic ranges. Such an approach would significantly improve the ability of the audiences listed here to connect with the complexities of displaying colonially aggregated collections in UK museums.

There can be concerns with this approach that some British audiences might be offended by criticism of national or family histories of colonialism required by these types of interpretation. Speaking of the feedback she received when promoting new forms of interpretation, Dr. Inbal Livne of the Powell-Cotton Museum noted:

> We had quite a few comments from local, white, visitors who didn't have a problem with the Museum's racist displays and therefore didn't see the need for change. It was helpful and heartening (and also disheartening!) to get lots of comments from other local non-visitors, who had been put off visiting precisely because of the colonial, racist, narratives – many of them Black, Indigenous or People of Colour who felt unwelcome. As a thread, these comments start to show the multiplicity of narratives that can be made, and seen, around the same collections. (pers. com.; see also, Livne, 2020)

Widening interpretation can therefore risk losing some British audiences, but with the possibility of engaging and attracting others who can improve the diversity in audience and opinion entering the museum space, as well as the knowledge that by acknowledging histories museums have historically avoided, museums are making ethical and progressive choices which will mitigate harm.

(3) Do Not Omit Complex Histories

To achieve this complexity, limit the scope to be able to present meaningful, detailed examinations of Native life rather than clumsy generalities: Taylor Norman was scathing about the failures this can bring.

> Honestly you can't display an entire continent of people within one gallery and do it justice and tell all the stories which need to be told; so many of the histories are so complex ... keep it as local as possible, even if it is telling the story of one family that's a story that is getting told ... stop trying to make things as big and broad and sweeping as possible and try to bring them in so that we can do these objects and their histories and their caretakers and the cultures that they come from justice. (Norman, 2019ii).

Norman's point here is that the collections did not originate with broad cultural groupings, often imposed externally onto diverse Indigenous peoples, but from specific localised environments. The collecting process has made it often very difficult to discern the minutiae of these environments, but by working with local communities and Indigenous curators it can become possible to narrow this down to the individual, and to tell real stories of real people.

Sarah Sense made much the same point, noting that the key was

> careful thinking about how institutions such as the British Museum could relate the objects in the collection back to the community and when possible an individual. Then, the exhibition would wake up a bit. It would have an opportunity to be a bit more engaging. Otherwise, what the institution does without making those connections is that it continues to cultivate stereotypes, and in some cases racism. If the exhibition is ultimately for education, then it's not doing a careful of job of educating – it's continuing colonial constructs. (Sense, 2019)

Sayet too notes this problem, and identifies that some UK museums, when discussing subjects closer to home, are capable of achieving this more effectively. She compared her experience of the display ethos at the Victoria & Albert Museum with the British Museum, noting that 'they set it up like you go on a journey, and its more theatrical. It's about your lived journey in relation to things. And I don't think there is any reason why the British Museum couldn't acknowledge what they had done and create an experience where you go on a lived journey in relationship to things' (Sayet, 2019ii).

A case study of this problem can be found in the Plains displays in the new Horniman Gallery, for while the Northwest Coast displays were praised, Native American Twitter was soon discussing the Plains case, pronouncing it 'Very problematic' in an online poll, in which there was particular concern that a suit of regalia was associated with a rifle and an explanatory text discussing Warrior Societies (Norman, 2019iii). Commentator Emmy Scott wrote, 'I can read the panel and honestly that makes it so much worse. It's a gross oversimplification of history and the warrior societies to glorify the savage warrior trope. They might as well put that Dior ad in there'[6] (Scott, 2019).

Taylor Norman, who visited the galley in person, described it as a 'dismal display', which gives

> a stereotypical presentation of Plains cultures- entrenched entirely in the Indian War era without recognition of how these cultures see personhood, giving or connection with the land... even in this well-intentioned attempt, the museum manages to erase women, along with amicable aspects of Plains culture unconnected to war and violence, and any description of who, most importantly, Indigenous people of the Plains are today... The omission of these factors suspends the museum's attempt at telling truths just short of being actual truth-telling because visitors are still largely left to maintain the false and /or stereotypical assumptions stemming from Hollywood portrayals... one relying on this display to educate could infer that Plains Natives are extinct given the limited time frame and subject matter. I need not launch into a discussion about the harm this causes. (Norman, 2019i:19)

Discussing it later at interview Norman noted, 'it was honestly shocking to me. I think the most shocking part of that is the mannequin in the middle holding the gun, just because it feels so violent. It feels violent, and it also goes with a theme I have been seeing – they focus on exclusively on warrior societies' (2019ii).

Even as here, in a gallery designed with Indigenous sensitivities in mind and which has engaged respectfully and productively with an Indigenous designer in another section of the display, the Plains case has inadvertently reinforced violent stereotypes of Native society to a British audience almost entirely lacking a contextual frame of reference. Had the display focused on specific communities or people, illustrating ordinary life not extraordinary exceptions, then it might have been a more focused and relatable experience for Norman – instead it presented a partial, alienating depiction of the cultures she had grown up around in a way which played directly into traumatising stereotypes.

---

[6] The Dior advert Scott mentions is a campaign which ran in the summer of 2019 for the Dior perfume *Sauvage,* heavily featuring Native American imagery and themes as well as the actor Johnny Depp (who controversially played a Native American character in the 2013 film *The Lone Ranger*). It, as the *New York Times* noted, '[set] off what seemed like a justifiable (and thus preventable) firestorm on social media thanks to the juxtaposition of Native American tradition and a word that sounded a lot like a historic racial slur.' The campaign was abandoned on 13 September (Friedman, 2019).

(4) Bring It Up to Date

Fourth, museums should bring the stories up to date and avoid talking about Native Americans as if they are dead and gone. Be sure to acknowledge the living cultures Tasi Baker discussed, and include material which shows how vibrant and alive Native American cultures are. Jenny Marlowe connects this with poor public education:

> A lot of folks have this sort of archival view of Native peoples – I think I said before people might be shocked at how many folks even in America just think that Native people died 500 years ago, or that if there are any, then they are all fakers or something like that. And there is a vacuum of education on the subject of Native peoples, so it is really rare to see any cultural institution engage with the idea of Native peoples as contemporary peoples, as living cultures. And I think ironically, because they are collections of the past, museums are uniquely positioned to do so, to display things and to put them in a context, a living context. (Marlowe, 2020)

Kainai actor Eugene Brave Rock recounted at interview that he had faced this lack of knowledge directly while filming in the UK. 'I remember somebody asking me who I was and I said I was a Native American and they honestly believed that we were all dead. They didn't actually think that I was Native American! And I wasn't going to argue with him' (Brave Rock, 2018). The background knowledge of Native American history in Britain is virtually non-existent, which means that museums have both a responsibility to portray it accurately, and an opportunity to educate from a space with minimal pre-existing prejudice.

This is not to say though that there is a lack of interest: Paula Peters of the Mashpee Wampanoag noted that in her encounters with British people there 'seemed to be a genuine interest. I feel that most of the people that I've dealt with in these various groups are very sincere about wanting to know more.' She identifies however that this enthusiasm isn't supported by education: 'what surprised me were the limitations of their knowledge ... But I imagine here there doesn't seem to be much of a focus [on education], because things we would expect them to know, they just don't know' (Peters, 2019). This is particularly true in knowledge about contemporary Native issues, which is almost non-existent outside academic circles.

Chris Andersen noted though that this was actually an aspect of the new Horniman World Galleries that worked well:

> The thing I really liked about the Horniman museum is the contemporariness of it. And I don't mean contemporariness as in they are keeping up with the arguments in the literature, I mean how far forward they actually come in

> displaying objects ... the narration of it, so that they put [them] into [their] social and political contexts and how far forward they were willing to go in terms of how they talked about it, [and] how some of the object-networks actually looked. (Andersen, 2019)

Engagement with the present should not of course mean that displays should avoid the genocidal history within which they were assembled, but by pretending that Native culture stopped when European collecting did is compounding the misrepresentation which those displays perpetrates – creating a fixed point between authentic and inauthentic imposed from an alien place of ignorance. Instead, museums should strive to make the galleries living spaces which give positive narratives about Indigenous recovery alongside the trauma. Taylor Norman noted this at interview:

> And our history – they don't choose to tell the happiest story right? It's about trying to keep culture alive in places where you know, either we weren't allowed to practice for a long time, or we didn't have access to right? But there is also potential for a story of hope. For example, it makes you happy when you see a little baby in a jingle dress dancing – it educates while showing our lives beyond trauma, and so it might not be the most traditional route of accessing culture, but it is still shared culture, its still something fun, its Native joy, it doesn't always have to be something heavy or spiritual in a cheapened way. (Norman, 2019ii)

Norman also talked about encountering a display from Standing Rock in a US museum and recognising objects from her own time at the protests and dissolving into tears: 'then I come to this museum and I see the post from Standing Rock and I lost it! I was like "Oh my God!" It was so powerful that I had to run to bathroom and collect myself a little bit.' Her personal history in a museum, one connected with an object, an event and a place of such power, helped contextualise the rest of the displays into a space of resilience through trauma – rather than trauma static and preserved – and the promotion thereby of Native joy (Norman, 2019ii).

Kwakwaka'wakw artist Sonny Assu, speaking of an artwork he produced which was exhibited and acquired by the Sainsbury Centre for Visual Arts, expressed hope that placing contemporary Indigenous American art into gallery spaces would both assist Native communities and artists and build legacies for the future:

> There's lots of contemporary artwork from the Pacific Northwest coast here in the UK, but I just hope it gives people, collectors and museums the understanding that this is a culture that is currently thriving in terms of an artistic standpoint, a culture that is, [that] Indigenous cultures from all over Northern America are, thriving and rising up, whether it's through art or

through activism, and that they're gonna start collecting these objects and put them on the mantle of Art . . . it's gonna feed this collection, it's gonna feed this notion of contemporary art. So that's really exciting. So I'm hoping that that future ancestor does come here and does discover these works and takes it in or uses it to learn from or study from or has their own resonancy and makes work in response to it whatever that might be in the future. (Assu, 2019)

Despite Assu's hopes, museums may not be able to acquire new material to update their collections due to budgetary and space concerns, but the use of imagery, video, sound and quotations, assembled in collaboration with Indigenous partners, are all achievable on limited budgets to illustrate to British audiences that the collections represent no more than a selective moment in the history of specific Native communities, rather than a fixed point of authenticity, and that the cultures from which they come are vibrant and alive.

2.3 No One Voice

These themes lie right at the heart of the fissure between museums and their Indigenous visitors. Native Americans understand explicitly that they are not homogenous, either as a collective or communally, as Sierra Tasi Baker points out: 'Indigenous people, tribe by tribe, are quite different, so it's really difficult to generalise us, no matter what, like I said, it's always a face to face conversation' (Tasi Baker, 2018), an individual, personal relationship. Native people live and work within tribes and broader groupings of peoples, but the vast majority of the objects from their peoples in museum collections do not stand for or represent them as a body. Instead they are collections of diverse and complicated individual stories of cultural experience, loss and survival intimately connected to the individual people who owned and cared for them.

But this is not all; in the *Indigenous Repatriation Handbook*, published open-access in 2019 and designed to demystify repatriation procedures for First Nations communities unused to museum bureaucracy, Jordan Coble, Indigenous curator at the Sncewips Heritage Museum, pointed out that these objects are not mere ciphers of the people to whom they once belonged, but active agents in their own right. He noted of the key to curation that 'It's honouring the artefacts as if they are living people. They have spirit to them. When people come into our museum, what we emphasise is that everything around us – and picture yourself in our museum right now – is alive' (Collison et al., 2019:12).

It is this shift which is so essential and so meaningful for effective engagement between museums, their British audiences and Indigenous American communities. Museums must step away from the curious spectacle of alien artefacts collected scientifically and shown off to visitors with their aesthetic qualities paramount. They must instead turn towards considering these collections as, in meaningful and essential ways, living non-human persons. As persons, they have rights, they have ambitions and they have loved ones, and can have meaningful effects on audiences in their own right if provided with the context to do so. They are not, therefore, detached objects of historical interest, isolated and remote, to be shaped according to non-Indigenous curatorial will, but travellers from distant lands, interconnected with the people from whom they came and as communicative and vibrant as their human contemporaries and forbears who left their own marks on Britain, some of whom even gave their lives and lie in British soil. In this capacity they evoke the same sense of loss, of disruption and colonial tragedy, but in their living condition – when this is facilitated and supported by the museum institution, which allows them space to breathe and live in the institution, which gives them access to voice and music and movement – they can enable transformative acts of collaborative reconciliation as they forge those historic connections anew with new generations of Indigenous and non-Indigenous visitors.

If these objects have rights, then those rights have to be understood and negotiated between the institutions which hold them and the communities from which they come. If they have ambitions and desires, then these too have to be understood and committed to as part of enduring partnerships between peoples. It must also be acknowledged that at time these ambitions might be to return to the homes from which they came, temporarily or permanently, and that their desires and ambitions might change over time. The question of who has the right to interpret these intentions on the part of these non-verbal non-humans is the contact zone conflict which has raged ever since Indigenous people began to revisit UK museums and to raise objections to the conditions in which these living beings are being kept. As Norman notes, appropriate 'Curation … respects object context, whether it be historical, physical, or transcendent, so as to work against the project of European standards onto non-European tangible heritage' (2019i).

Though there are substantial historical imbalances to overcome and traumas to mitigate, the conclusion from the interviews *Beyond the Spectacle* has conducted points to the critical importance of a future collaborative approach, which places Indigenous knowledge at the centre of the mediation between the collections, the institutions and the British public in whose trust they are maintained. This will have multiple effects: It will provide better and more nuanced public education in Britain about the legacies of colonialism and the peoples for whom it was so destructive. It will enable museums to better care for the collections for which they are physically responsible in ways more respectful and effective towards the objects and the peoples from which they came. It will give the objects themselves more opportunity to exist within the contexts for which they were originally made, and within which they still resonate.

Perhaps most importantly, it will create a space in which British conversations about decolonisation, repatriation, reengagement and reinterpretation can be held collaboratively and on a stable long-term footing, giving those Indigenous visitors to collections, for whom they mean the most, a sense of place and intimacy near impossible under current conditions and giving British audiences new Indigenous-led viewpoints. The critical question of the following section is to ask to what extent such a situation is possible in the face of the twin crises facing museums in the third decade of the twenty-first century.

3 The Twin Crises: British Ethnographic Collections in the Twenty-First Century

Truth-telling works to alter discourse and, for truth-telling to occur, marginalized voices must be present.

Taylor Norman, Mvskoke (2019i:19)

This section examines the two largest problems the UK museum sector faces in its curation of ethnographic collections in the twenty-first century, which I am calling the crisis of representation, and the crisis of expertise. This time is a liminal point of change in the curatorial profession, change driven by two major factors which I term here the twin crises. These crises, intertwined and exacerbating one another, are fundamentally reshaping the role of museums in the UK and the ways in which they are run, overturning centuries of sometimes stifling tradition in a transition both rapid and almost entirely unplanned. The result will fundamentally realign how museums operate in Britain, particularly museums with ethnographic collections, with serious ramifications for public education, collections care management and display and the ethical and cultural assumptions which underpin the entire sector.

The first crisis is a growing call for greater and more meaningful representation in the museum space by marginalised and colonised peoples whose material culture forms so much of these collections. Emanating externally, and often at a distance from the museum institution, this crisis is growing in volume and critical mass, absorbed into the wider cultural wars between progressive and conservative factions in society which define so much of contemporary political dialogue. The second crisis is an unanticipated change in the very expertise which underpins the curatorial role, accelerated by significant changes in the funding models by which UK museums operate. At the heart of these crises is constant debate about which audiences museums should be for, from where they derive their authority and how they balance between the disparate audiences to whom they cater.

Museums in Britain, and particularly ethnographic museums, are conglomerations primarily of their own histories rather than the histories of other peoples in other places. They are assemblages of disparate items drawn together at whim by Georgian and Victorian scholars and enthusiasts intending to create institutions which would enable British scholars to study the world and to educate the British public about the results of those studies. They have thus, through most of their history, been not so much a repository of foreign histories, but a haphazard and selective synthesis of the world through our own. As Collections and Engagement Curator (Human History) at Hastings Museum Eleanor Lanyon identified: 'what they chose to collect, trade, steal, or whatever, reflects their view of the world rather than the view of the people whose cultural heritage they were appropriating, so we may never be able to tell a rounded story because they only collected certain things. They collected things because they looked nice, or they backed up their preconceptions' (Hastings, 2019). As in the Horniman Plains displays, and as former British Museum Curator Jonathan King noted, in the case of Native Americans this selective collecting means that 'as a result, the most traumatic period in Native American history has provided the material basis for what is traditional and what is not' (King, 1986:70).

Enlightenment philosophies, with their inherently problematic racial, social and cultural biases, lie at the very core of the foundation of most culture museums in the UK. But the Enlightenment was not only confined to the minds and libraries of European scholars – its greatest period was also that in which the Empires of Northern Europe, and in particular that of Britain, expanded exponentially. Empires dedicated to trade and driven by scientific and pseudoscientific principles rapidly spread to every corner of the globe, expansion sustained by relentless and irresistible military, paramilitary and economic force. As they expanded, the European powers fought internecine wars between one another in pursuit of mercantile and political supremacy, and myriad colonial conflicts with the original inhabitants of those spaces for dominance over land and resources.

Although Imperial propaganda often liked to paint the British Empire as a fatherly shepherd watching over a wayward flock, the British Empire and its European brethren were not of course benign or benevolent institutions. Everywhere empires spread, local governments were overthrown in favour of political or mercantile interests, and in the process their populations were displaced, enslaved and all too often, massacred. To facilitate the processes of replacement and assimilation, religions, traditions and ways of life were deliberately and systematically exterminated to make way for colonial governance in order to ensure the reliable and consistent transfer of wealth from the colonies to the Imperial centre. The litany of plague, famine and war which these Enlightenment Empires wrought has left an inescapable legacy imprinted onto the map and the people of the world today.

Museums in Britain, for all their scientific pretensions, were not only not apart from this process, they were at the very heart of the philosophical justifications for the expansion of Empire. As the process of colonial assimilation caused objects from across the world to aggregate in their halls, they were understood as scientific collections or reference libraries of zoological and human material culture, cataloguing the world as had been and was rapidly becoming. These collections, though developed with a pseudoscientific ambition for completeness, were by their very nature imperfect, incomplete and assembled with knowing Eurocentric bias. As public institutions, they simultaneously however became the dumping ground for the curiosities and eccentricities of the conquered world, part laboratory, part fairground freak show, all driven by the aesthetic tastes of collectors and curators drawn exclusively from the British social elite. It was in this mould that in the late nineteenth century they became the breeding ground of pseudo-Darwinian theories of cultural evolution which excused the subjugation of non-European peoples on racial grounds, as proposed in the works of Sir Francis Galton, the father of eugenics, or Augustus Pitt-Rivers, who founded the principles of evolutionary archaeology and established a museum at the University of Oxford to promote his ideas which still bears his name and imprint.

Today these theories are long debunked, and despite a stubborn retention in parts of the general public, they have little credence in mainstream academia and modern museum display. However, British museums in the twenty-first century are forced to continually grapple with this legacy in their work with the collections they own, both in the composition of the collections themselves, and in tired but still visible legacies of their historic use and display. The evidence of this historic museum complicity and engagement in the harm of colonialism is, as this project's research demonstrates, ever-present in the collections they hold and the histories which accompany those collections. As Jenny Marlowe noted at interview, this history affects and informs the way she looks at museums, considering 'how museums have colonially taken things out of their context and put them on shelves and charged white people money to look at them.' (Marlowe, 2020). Marlowe points out here that museums have not just benefitted in the past from colonial extractive collecting, but are still benefiting right now.

How museums engage with the modern communities from whose ancestors these collections were extracted is a critical part of contemporary curation and doing so in an ethical and respectful manner is an essential skill, one made significantly more complex by the twin crises, both uncontrolled and deeply impactful on the sector, which are outlined in this section. These crises, the representation crisis created by the demands from Indigenous peoples for greater authority not only over physical ownership of collections, but of how they are used under museum ownership, and the expertise crisis of the increasing generalisation of the skills of museum professionals in the UK, which leads to gaps in knowledge on how to appropriately engage with peoples marginalised by history. Dividing these crises, this section examines how each has come about and its impact on both on the minutiae of curatorial collections management, as well as its contribution to an increasingly concerning cultural divide between those who would acknowledge the past and mitigate its harm and those who would deny the past and thus exacerbate the damage it continues to cause.

3.1 Evolving Ethics

In early 2019, a wave of statements backing initiatives by museum authorities and governments across Europe expressed new willingness to engage with former colonial states and Indigenous groups on the issue of access, control and repatriation of colonially assembled museum collections. Though this wave is the product of decades of activism, scholarship and collaboration, it gained its most recent impetus from statements in 2017 by the then–newly elected French President Emmanuel Macron. Macron's remarks were based on a groundbreaking report by Bénédicte Savoy and Felwine Sarr which examined the best future course for French museums holding collections from the French colonial Empire, particularly from Africa, in improving the representation and display of those collections and connecting effectively with the nations and communities from which they came.

The recommendations of this report were for sweeping reforms to the processes of Indigenous representation and repatriation within the museum sector, based on a movement towards reversing the presumption that European museum institutions should be the principle home of these collections, to one which assumes their countries of origin must be the default institutions best able to care for and interpret them. Savoy wrote, 'There should be no conditions attached to the restitutions, we are dealing with the case of a continent which has almost nothing left of its history when we have it all. The aim is not to empty Western museums to fill up the African ones, but to invent a new relationship based on ethics and equity' (Noce, 2018; Adams, 2018).

Macron himself was unequivocal about implementing the report's provisions: 'Starting today, and within the next five years, I want to see the conditions put in place so as to allow for the temporary or definitive restitution of African cultural heritage to Africa' (Sarr & Savoy, 2018).

The Savoy/Sarr report does not however present this process as one which can be completed without complexity. It acknowledges that there are not only competing interests at stake with substantial investment riding on the outcome, but also that the people engaged in the conversation are themselves products of the colonial period and its deeply entangled histories. In its conclusion, the report notes crucially that:

> These objects which for a large part have been ripped away from their cultures of origin by way of colonial violence, but which were welcomed and cared for by generations of curators in their new places of residence, from now on bear within them an irremediable piece of Europe and Africa. Having incorporated several regimes of meaning, they become sites of the creoliza-tion of cultures and as a result they are equipped to serve as mediators of a new relationality. (Sarr & Savoy, 2018:87)

It acknowledges here, succinctly and clearly, that the debate on Indigenous access to and control of collections of imperially assembled objects is a complex negotiation of not only the power relations within the museum contact zone, but of new 'creolized', or hybridised, cultural groupings forming from the colonial period and represented and reflected directly in the museum space and the arguments and collaborations which surround it.

Following the French lead, other governments and museum authorities in Europe took up the initiative Macron had laid down. In March 2019, the Dutch National Museum of World Cultures, an umbrella body managing the major Dutch colonial collections, launched new policy guidelines which put the emphasis and initiative for repatriation and access debates onto former colonies and Indigenous nations and promising, among other things, a maximum time-frame of one year to settle repatriation claims. Most crucially, the policy sought to retrospectively apply contemporary law onto historic acquisitions. Director Stijn Schoonderwoerd gave a statement on the collection:

> It is certain that we manage objects that the original owner did not relinquish of his own accord. In these cases, claims are justified in our eyes. If today we say that on the basis of international treaties, objects stolen from Syria do not belong in our collection, then why should that principle not apply to objects stolen 100 years ago? (Hickley, 2019i)

In the same week that the new Dutch policy was launched, a collaborative group of sixteen German regional culture ministers issued their own agreement on promoting and facilitating repatriation discussions, with a focus on improving and standardising documentation. They also sought to establish a national body to which prospective repatriation claims might be made and processed, in order to streamline and systematise the mechanisms by which Indigenous groups could discover, access and engage with the collections and ultimately formalise their claims. Their inspiration came directly from Macron's speech, with Jürgen Zimmerer of the University of Hamburg noting that 'Germany has missed the chance to make a big political gesture like France, but this document shows it is taking the subject very seriously' (Hickley, 2019ii).

The momentum on the European continent in addressing the historical imbalances of colonially assembled museum collections is thus clearly in favour of continued engagement, greater and more extensive Indigenous representation and streamlined progressive repatriation initiatives. There have been and will continue to be missteps and controversies, as distinctly mixed reviews for the African Museum in Brussels, opened in December 2018, show. It was criticised for its inconsistent approach to the legacies of Belgian colonialism, but more significantly for failing to engage with the acknowledgements identified in the previous section by Jenny Marlowe: 'A greater shortcoming is that nothing here really links the exploitation of the Congo's riches … with Belgium's own prosperity … A good museum should make you start looking at the world beyond its walls with new eyes' (Hochschild, 2020). The sense remaining therefore is that reconciliation can take place in museums only, rather than operating as part of a wider, coordinated movement of public education and acknowledgement. Despite missteps and missed opportunities however, there is a recent but clear trajectory in Europe towards more effective collaborative acknowledgement of colonial pasts in the senior management levels of major European cultural institutions.

In Britain however there is far less national coordination on these issues, within a sector which has been slow to respond to the crisis affecting it, particularly though major cultural institutions. Individually there are signs that parts of the sector are acknowledging and engaging with some of the more egregious examples of colonial looting, particularly with regard to human remains. In 2019 alone, for example, the Natural History Museum authorised the return of thirty-seven ancestral remains to Australia; the National Museum of Scotland has agreed to return two Beothuk skulls to Canada; and the Bristol Museum has returned two Tongva skulls, excavated from a gravesite on the Californian Channel Islands in the late nineteenth century, to the Ti'at Society, a Tongva organisation actively pursuing repatriation claims.

In late 2019, both the Arts Council England and the Museums Association established working groups to examine these issues and work towards creating effective guidance and policy for museums, but their efforts are comparatively conservative and small-scale when faced with the more sweeping changes in other European countries, and there has been a push back, particularly in some quarters of the national press: in February 2020, Professor Nigel Biggar of Christ Church, Oxford, asked rhetorically and scathingly 'is everybody who descends from those who were once enslaved or colonised still being harmed by those now ancient and distant misdeeds?' (2020). Though Biggar clearly believes they are not, his fundamental and very Eurocentric misapprehensions of the words 'ancient' and 'distant' to refer to events that for Indigenous peoples the world over are neither, betrays a closely held belief within institutional and academic hierarchies that, contrary to Savoy and Sarr's conclusions, the former centres of Imperial power remain the appropriate place for authority over ethnographic collections to reside.

As a result, on a broader sectoral or institutional level, the encouraging collaborations listed previously are anomalies. It is noticeable, for example, that these repatriations only and specifically concern human remains, not any of the many thousands of material culture objects in collections which have similarly questionable provenance and about which Macron spoke and on which Sarr and Savoy focused. In common with Biggar's article, recent public interventions on the subject by some of the most senior museum professionals in Britain demonstrate limited understanding of the nuances of the current debate or any sense of urgency with regard to promoting, discussing or settling the issues at hand.

In April 2018, in an interview for the *Guardian*, Hartwig Fisher, Director of the British Museum, reiterated a newly nuanced version of the museum's long-held stance that its collections are 'universal', a display of the world for the world. He said that 'Whoever comes in here and crosses the threshold is not a foreigner. There are no foreigners here. This is a world country, this museum. While at the same time we recognise that this is a British creation, to which the cultures of all the world have contributed.' Challenged on this benign assessment of what has always fundamentally been a colonial project of capturing and seriating – dividing and cataloguing – the world, he countered that 'I always say what has been created here, which is open to everybody, creates an extraordinary opportunity to see cultural heritage in a context you have in only a very few places. That is the museum's major value and it is very precious' (Higgins, 2018).

A year later, in an interview for a Greek newspaper, Fisher expanded this idea. He noted that in relation to the highly controversial Parthenon Friezes, 'We should appreciate this opportunity [to have them in London]. You could, of course, be saddened by the fact that the original environment has disappeared. When you move a cultural heritage to a museum, you move it outside. However, this shifting is also a creative act' (Brown, 2019). Although later claimed by a spokesperson as 'the longstanding position of the British Museum', and predictably drawing criticism from Greek cultural institutions, this statement actually further marks a departure in the museum's rhetoric, from self-proclaimed safeguard of the world's heritage, to the melting pot within which something entirely new and, crucially, sufficiently divorced from its original context to inhibit repatriation, is supposedly created.

As the largest and most prominent participant in the repatriation controversy in Britain, the British Museum is a taste leader within and without the sector. Drawing on this newly introduced (to the public debate) notion of the seizure and accumulation of cultural heritage from around the world as a creative act, one which turns the objects from something old to something new (and consequently, something British), other commentators, writing in support of Fisher, have put the issue more starkly. A few months later, Tristram Hunt, Director of the Victoria and Albert Museum, wrote in the *Guardian* that 'There remains something essentially valuable about the ability of museums to position objects beyond particular cultural or ethnic identities' (2019), implying that merely by being in the museum and subject to museum control, objects had lost some essential part of what made them part of Indigenous or non-European cultures and had taken on a European quality which made them now newly created European objects for museum display.

This is hardly a new theoretical position; it echoes Kryzrof Pomian's (1990) theory of museum objects as semiophores, objects which by entering a museum space become stripped of economic value and substituted with representational value. Yet neither Fisher nor Hunt expressed any concern or appreciation in their interventions that this might for some people, particularly those people from whom the objects were removed, or their descendants, be a destructive act. They do not acknowledge that by recreating objects in this way museums are constantly recapitulating acquisitive colonialist actions into the twenty-first century in ways which may potentially cause serious harm to the colonised communities from which they come.

Between these interventions, art critic Jonathan Jones published an opinion piece, also in the *Guardian*, which stated clearly the new case against repatriation being constructed in the national media: 'if you don't see [Fisher's] case, you are ultimately saying there shouldn't be any world museums and every work of art should stay in its original location, as it only has meaning in its original context' and 'those who argue for the return of the Parthenon sculptures and any other such restitution need to be clear that in attacking the dream of the world museum you are assaulting the heritage of the Enlightenment' (Jones, 2019).

Jones's strident position in a national newspaper thus deliberately establishes the straw-man debate as between an unnuanced blanket repatriation and the entirety of modern Western liberal thought, as embodied in the Enlightenment which spawned and was partially sustained by encyclopaedic museums such as the British Museum. Indeed, logically it goes further, for if repatriation is an assault on the European heritage of Enlightenment, then so by extension is any non-European interpretation or representation in the gallery space, or ultimately any non-European voice which offers criticism of this narrow interpretation of European history. Professor Robert Janes has summarily dismissed such arguments as no more than 'a post-hoc rationalization that sustains a colonial past or a new chapter in colonial history dressed up in contemporary parlance' (Janes, 2015:15), but inevitably it took almost no time at all for this line of argument to be used by Conservative Culture Secretary Jeremy Wright to dismiss the notion of repatriation out of hand (Sanderson, 2019).

Wright, a man with no professional museum background or education, argued that if museums 'followed the logic of restitution to its logical conclusion' ultimately Britain would have 'no single points where people can see multiple things', and attempted to shift the debate, criticising the entire premise of contested ownership and suggesting instead that representation was the greater issue; 'Never mind the argument about who owns this thing, let's argue about how it gets to be seen' (Hatfield, 2019), deliberately obscuring that repatriation and representation are entangled and inseparable parts of the same decolonisation argument.

Wright's statement was criticised by the Museums Association, the professional body which provides a loose organisational structure within which museum practice in the UK can be standardised, with Director Sharon Heal noting, 'This kind of thinking flies in the face of the informed conversation about decolonisation, restitution and repatriation that is taking place in the sector in the UK and at government level in many countries in Europe' (Heal, 2019), but it remains the UK government position for the foreseeable future, and forms the landscape within which curators and institutions seeking to nuance and mitigate the potential for harm within their collections must navigate.

There is much that is problematic with the approach of scholars and cultural leaders like Biggar, Fisher, Hunt, Jones and Wright, who seek to reiterate the formal redesignation of these objects from Indigenous material culture to European material culture by virtue of formal legal ownership and claims to have remade the objects through their acquisition. Not least problematic among the counterarguments is the salient point, made, for example, in a March 2019 article by historian Emma Lundin, that the UK's 'hostile environment' visa conditions promoted by the government of which Wright is a part prevent the overwhelming majority of the world's population from viewing the collections, effectively undermining the argument that a new suite of objects has been truly laid before the world's people in these institutions (Lundin, 2019).

The Museums Association has, and promoted in its response, its own Code of Ethics, last revised in 2015, which attempts to provide a framework by which museums can navigate these ethical and legal conflicts. However, this document provides nothing more than a simple sound bite on this critical issue. The relevant text, in its entirety, is from paragraph 2.7; 'Deal sensitively and promptly with requests for repatriation both within the UK and from abroad' (Museums Association, n.d.)

This advice, though no doubt well meant, does not help provide nuance or complexity to the implications of millions of historical decisions which comprise the provenance details of the vast ethnographic collections in UK museums. More detail is given in the recent Empowering Collections Report, which works to improve representation in museum interpretation, but this too is a slight document in the face of such a towering issue. Point two in this document addresses this concern, alongside a case study, noting that museums need:

> *A proactive approach to the democratisation and decolonisation of museums*
> Collections are increasingly contested by different groups in society. Many museums have sought to play a positive role in these discussions, but there is a lack of information about how to approach issues related to decolonisation and restitution. Sector support organisations, the MA Ethics Committee and museums should work together to establish new guidance for the sector and ensure that museums take a proactive approach in the reinterpretation and decolonising of collections. (Museums Association, 2019)

Guidance is reportedly being developed through 2020, and may change the landscape when it is published, but it has to date been sorely lacking. In 2019, the museum sector in Britain faces the two simultaneous existential crises which began this section, the 'representation crisis' and the 'expertise crisis' which, separately and especially in combination, stand to permanently alter the fundamental nature of the role and service museums provide.

3.2 The Representation Crisis

The representation crisis concerns the increasing volume and tenacity with which Indigenous peoples, and particularly those who were or are subject to colonisation by European empires, are demanding redress through museum spaces.

Museums in the UK are home to vast collections of material, both man-made and natural history, which do not all originate in Britain. Whether collected archaeologically, zoologically or ethnographically, many of these collections were assembled by the passage of British (and more broadly European) peoples away from Europe and out into the rest of the world as part of the conquest and colonisation by European nations over a period running approximately from the early sixteenth century to the mid-twentieth century. This ostentatious military, religious and economic imperialism was accompanied by a subtler cultural and scientific imperialism which has come to be known collectively as a crucial part of the European Enlightenment and whose effects, while no-less pernicious to the Indigenous populations it touched, are far less well understood and critiqued today outside academia.

In many cases, most dramatically that of Augustus Pitt-Rivers, whose ensuing eponymous museum remains one of the most important such institutions in Britain, these collections were assembled and displayed with the express intention of promoting an explicitly white-supremacist view of human civilisation. In others, this outcome was more inadvertent, and yet in every institution these underlying assumptions about the technological and cultural superiority of Europe directly impacted both the internal conversation of and the external education provided by these institutions.

This history is still not well represented in museums: Elizabeth Edwards has criticised the 'near complete absence of an engagement with colonial enterprise and colonial collecting . . . The colonial past is tidily sequestrated into a series of "elsewhere" so as to avoid the responsibility to engage with its implications – it happened a long time ago (really?), a long way away (really?) or that it is a "problem" confined to ethnographic collections (really?)' (2018).

The result is that these so-called 'recreated' objects are not only owned but controlled by the museum, alienated from their original communities and used as representatives of entire cultures in ways which are often reliant on stereotypes which exacerbate the harm caused by the colonial contexts in which these collections were assembled.

3.3 Remaking Objects

As Fisher noted, the process of acquisition recreates objects, both individually and *en masse*, and has turned objects from existing within a very specific time and place into ostensibly universal, theoretically recreated objects of representation, known as semiophores. It does not however mean that this process of re-creation is an effective argument against repatriation. On the contrary, it suggests that the entire acquisitive process of the museum environment is one which has corrosively entrenched the kind of colonised mind-set which is causing the representation crisis in the first place.

Visiting an ancestor in the British Museum collection, Haida delegate Gaahlaay Lonnie Young said

> I'd want [people] to support our ancestor coming home. Why won't they allow us to repatriate our ancestors when they're not even being studied? They've been in storage for so long and they haven't done anything. Why don't people in museums let them go? I think most societies, or most peoples, would like that. That's what I want to see come out of this process – our people home again. The art – the art is for everybody. But our people belong at home with us. (Krmpotich & Peers, 2013:224)

As of the time of writing in 2020, the ancestor remains in a British Museum storage facility.

Young's comments, by contrast with Fisher's theories of remaking objects in the museum, is emblematic of the way in which the calls for museums decolonisation – repatriation and representation – from marginalised and colonised peoples are growing stronger yet not being consistently acted upon in the museum sector. They demand not just good-faith conversations about repatriation, the return of certain objects to original communities and contexts, but as Alice Procter has noted, also a meaningful say in how the objects which remain exist within the museum (Procter, 2019). Repatriation is not itself enough to successfully decolonise the museum space, since the erasure of marginalised peoples there is no less a colonially imposed injustice than their insertion without consent, but it is a critical and highly contentious first stage.

Beyond the return of objects though, these calls for representation demand not just a say in how Indigenous collections in European museums are displayed and stored, but actual, direct and meaningful agency over these collections, such that they become not recontextualised props for representing alien cultures to an ill-informed European public, but a collaborative, mutually beneficial communication between Indigenous peoples and museum visitors. Section 3 of this Element will explore in greater depth the techniques by which this might be achieved, but the reality is that this seems to be less likely and more at risk in Britain than ever before, and the reason for this is the second of the twin crises of this section, the expertise crisis.

3.4 The Expertise Ccrisis

Since 2010, there has been a dramatic, unplanned and seismic shift in how employment in the museum sector is constituted. Historically, museums in the

United Kingdom have been curatorially led, with decisions on significant matters made by professional academic curators with subject specialisms. This is the model first laid down in those Enlightenment scientific institutions of the eighteenth century, in which subject experts with years of scholarly training and publication ran specialist collections as research resources.

Even at smaller institutions, where there were not the resources to hire specific experts for specific collections, the curators were experts in something – their remit might spread across many parts of the world and long time periods, but there was generally an area among these options in which they had specific expertise which could be extrapolated more widely. Moreover, these curators often stayed in position for decades, in dual supervisory roles as curator and collection manager, and thus became intimately acquainted with the specifics of particular collections, their histories and the people for whom they were especially important.

After 2010, accumulating cuts to budgets meant that this employment model became unsustainable across the sector. As budgets fell year on year, sector leaders began to warn that the consequences would fundamentally change the nature of museum management. David Fleming, the President of the Museums Association, warned in 2015, that 'one of the inevitable consequences of budget cuts is that museums will have to adjust the way they work' (Sullivan, 2015).

So severe has the cumulative effect of cuts to the museum sector been, that an independent report, the Mendoza Review, was commissioned in 2017 to examine the state of the sector and recommend adjustments to managerial structures and outreach to cope with the changes in funding and organisation. The Mendoza Review reported, somewhat disingenuously, that museum funding ultimately had remained 'consistent' in the years 2008–17, but without inflation adjustments the amount available had fallen on average by 13 per cent. Moreover, this statistic disguises how severe these cuts have been at specific and crucial points of the sector, particularly in local authority museums. A case study within the report reflects that Derby Museums, for example, suffered 30 per cent cuts to funding between 2015 and 2017 alone, and as a result was forced to move from a local authority museum to an independent charitable trust, reliant almost entirely on precarious charitable-support funding from local industries for its maintenance and future (Mendoza, 2017). Between 2010 and 2015, one in five museums outside London had experienced temporary closures due to insufficient funding, and forty-four have been closed permanently (Brown, 2016). This is not, to put it mildly, evidence of consistent funding.

The report does also however illustrate the nature of the problem. It demonstrates that the remaining sources of governmental funding, and consequently the purposes for which it can be used, are far more restricted than before 2010, with reductions in routine central and local government funding supplemented by grants from Heritage Lottery Fund (HLF), the Association for Cultural Enterprises (ACE) and other bodies. These funds are by their very nature, unevenly accessible; for example, almost half of HLF funding goes to museums in London, which comprise just 11 per cent of the nation's total. In addition, they cannot generally be used for long-term running and staffing costs, only for shorter-term project work, leaving core funding disproportionally hit by cuts with the result that museum employment is rapidly shifting from permanent secure jobs to short-term, precarious work directed at peripheral rather than core operations (Mendoza, 2017). In 2015, a quarter of museums reported cuts to permanent staffing levels and nearly half of museums were attempting to fill the staffing vacancies with unpaid volunteers, greatly increasing instability in sector staffing (Brown, 2016).

One of the most dramatic examples of this type of staff rationalisation came at Leicester. In 2019, Leicester City Council arts and museum service made all four of their expert curators redundant at once, replacing them with seven staff in roles, including 'exhibitions and displays manager, a digital project manager, a children and young people's officer, a community engagement officer and collections access officer' as part of an 'arts, museums, festivals and events team'. This is no longer a museum as originally understood as a place of curation, research and learning, but an educational events team, professionally trained in engagement but without expert knowledge of the materials with which they will be working. Unsurprisingly, there were complaints at this unconsulted move, with an unnamed member of the public presciently pointing out in the *Leicester Mercury* that, 'there will come a point where nobody within the service will have knowledge of the very collections they hold' (Orton, 2019).

Museums up and down the country have been affected by this process, as redundancies and retirements leave curatorial posts unstaffed and temporary contracts are used to patch gaps, resulting in inconsistency and a loss of accumulated knowledge. A side effect of this has been the actions in a few institutions of using disposal practices by governing bodies to raise funding through unethical means. The Mendoza Report recommends 'collection rationalisation', by which they mean planning for the disposal of collections peripheral to the museum's main function which the museum can no longer afford to support. As the report notes, the Museums Association has clear guidance on how 'rationalisation' can be achieved ethically to ensure that publicly owned historical collections are not dispersed into the private sector, out of public ownership or engagement – that publicly owned assets remain publicly owned.

In a few places however local authorities have simply ignored these guidelines, selling important collections on the open market and seizing the profits for other projects. One example was the sale of the Riesco Collection at Croydon Museum in 2013, for which the museum was stripped of Arts Council England Accreditation and was, in the words of Museums Association Director Mark Taylor, 'casting itself into cultural wilderness' (Steel, 2013) This has significant implications for the representation crisis; how much worse it is for museums to be seen to be profiting from unethically obtained objects, than to hold them in care with the potential for return.

That this sort of activity has been made possible by the cuts to museum funding described above is an extreme but perhaps inevitable example of the type of outcome caused by the expertise crisis in museum governance. Museums across the sector have lost staff in huge numbers, and losses are concentrated in particular among the most experienced, long-serving staff. Their replacements are a different sort of curator; professionally trained non-specialist curators who rarely come via other academic disciplines and are instead prepared for their positions via museum studies masters programmes and experience outside academia.

These courses provide an excellent grounding in museum history and theory and high-quality vocational training in the management of a museum and the communication of its main ideas to the audience. Damian Etherington of Hastings Museum notes that this is 'a response to the outcomes required by strategic funders which by and large drive participation and engagement over other outcomes which is compounded by the production of degree-educated museum professionals whose experience/knowledge is not grounded in an academic specialism – not that this is a bad thing, it needs a balanced approach to make it work' (pers. com.).

This balance is however currently lacking, in part because these training courses do not always provide sufficient engagement with issues of Indigenous representation, and rarely facilitate actual experience with Indigenous visitors. Crucially, the new curators are not usually experts in subjects beyond the museum as an institution itself, and consequently their curatorial work is reflective of this lack of specialist knowledge, catering more than ever to the reactions of British visitors (for whom they have been trained), than their Indigenous visitors (for whom they have not), and operating with the dominant colonial ethos of the museum, even in cases where their personal sympathies may lie with decolonisation efforts.

This description of the sector thus far is not intended as an indictment of museum studies masters programmes or their graduates – crucial components of modern and effective museology within the sector – nor is it to attack the new generation of curators, hard-working and underpaid, who are adapting to this unplanned landscape of short-term contracts and minimal and unstable funding. Rather, it is intended as an indictment of the failures in strategic funding and management which have led to the expertise crisis, and a reflection of concern at the speed at which the profession is changing and the rate at which experience and subject-specialist expertise is being replaced by younger, more-generalist staff not acquainted with the particular problems found in the curation of ethnographic collections.

Without the depth of experience and knowledge passed hand-to-hand down curatorial generations, museums across Britain are not only losing existing relationships and resources, they are increasingly losing the ability to recognise what their collections even hold. Without subject specialists, the cultural nuances around specific objects and collections and the communities from which they come are more likely to be missed, and opportunities to engage collaboratively with the growing and increasingly mobile and vocal generation of modern Indigenous activists will be lost, with significant risks for the museums involved.

Museums which fail to engage meaningfully with Indigenous communities, educators and the resources they produce will inevitably face consequences, not only damaging the museum's reputation both with the public and its peers, but also potentially triggering exactly the type of trauma described in the first section for Indigenous partners, or potential partners. Neither individual heritage institutions, nor the wider sector, can afford for such trauma to become routine, nor to become pawns in wider culture-war antagonisms which will only entrench bad practice and bad history.

On Sunday, 7 June 2020, the statue of slave-trader Edward Colston, which had stood in Bristol since 1895, was torn down and thrown into Bristol harbour as part of UK-wide Black Lives Matter protests. The statue had been the subject of repeated campaigns to remove it or better contextualise it for a public audience, but opponents of removal had blocked or watered down every effort, including a suggestion that the statue be removed to Bristol Museum. By refusing to listen to those who were caused suffering by the presence of the statue of the man responsible for such violence and pain, by failing to mitigate or meaningfully acknowledge the trauma the statue causes, and the straightforward ethics of celebrating a slave trader in twenty-first-century Britain, its supporters sealed its fate: it was later dragged from the harbour and deposited at the museum, its future uncertain. A few days later, African activists entered the Quai Branly Museum in Paris and attempted to remove artefacts from display with the intent of repatriating them. Museums in Britain must take note – if they will not or do not listen to the representation crisis, if they cannot decolonise, actively promoting healing through collaboration and reconciliation, the opportunity may be taken from them.

3.5 Indigenous Encounters

The Mendoza Review does not mention the representation crisis. Such consideration was not perhaps within its remit, but the omission of this burgeoning issue in relation to funding and staff cuts and an ensuing deficit in expertise in Indigenous relations indicates perhaps that the issue is not yet taken seriously enough across the sector, particularly in terms of the potential catastrophes which may emerge as these two crises collide with one another over the next few decades.

This debate is dominated of course by the question of repatriation, the physical return of museum collections to communities of origin. This clouds all other discussion, hanging over the conversation and obscuring the nuances which lie at the heart of effective decolonisation: the mitigation of harm. Some collections, no doubt, were obtained illegally and should be returned. Others are legally more problematic, but still subject to clear ethical considerations pertaining to ownership. But yet more, indeed the vast majority of ethnographic assemblages in Britain, are assembled through unequal colonial modes of trade and exchange, lying between outright theft and large-scale cultural coercion.

The argument over whether this body of material should or should not be repatriated has hardly yet begun, but it is inevitable that the bulk of it will remain, its histories leaving it either unclaimable, or its communities uninterested in reclaiming it. The rest of this Element speaks to all such collections, but with a particular focus on Native American groups as some of the most prominent, vocal and outspoken participants in the representation crisis, but whose voices, with some exceptions, have so far not been well represented in the critical literature in Britain.

In the section that follows, I have developed, with sector and Indigenous partners, a policy guideline to assist museum staff unfamiliar with the issues discussed here on how to navigate their relationships with Indigenous peoples and communities. These are designed so that museums can adapt them into formal policy, reviewed and approved by governing bodies and written into museum practice for the future, so that staffing changes or shifts in the ways in which museums are run and managed do not inhibit ongoing ethical engagement between Indigenous communities and the museums which own their heritage.

4 Designing Policy

The Element has so far explored the current state of theoretical and cultural debate in Britain within the context of the twin crises threatening to overwhelm museums which own and display collections from Indigenous colonised peoples from around the world. It has also illustrated just how damaging the experience of visiting these museums can be for the descendants of the peoples who made these objects and endured the colonial periods in which they were removed.

There is sometimes in museum circles a fear that making radical changes of approach, particularly those which deliberately favour parts of the museum's audience – as Indigenous access policies inevitably do – can alienate much more frequent non-Indigenous visitors. However, recent efforts by the Powell-Cotton Museum, a museum developed from the colonial African collections of Percy Powell-Cotton, to express support and make changes in approach have demonstrated that these fears are best addressed directly.

Inbal Livne, Head of Collections and Engagement, responded to a query into public responses:

> We did, initially, get a lot of comments telling us we should be 'ashamed of whitewashing history' and should 'leave the past in the past'. We made sure to answer every one of those comments thoughtfully and positively. Answering those comments in a way that doesn't seek to demean or embarrass those individuals but equally doesn't let them off being prejudicial, has increased support for our project by showing we are keen to hear and respond to all comments and not just those we agree with … Ultimately those who continue to find our change in narrative a problem, do so because they have a problem. As an institution we have taken the decision that its okay if we lose some support from those who do not feel able to come on this journey with us. Sometimes doing the right thing is just more important. (pers.com.2020)

Museums therefore need not be afraid that engaging with new audiences and modes of communication which reflect Indigenous vales will alienate British audiences – professional education and engagement will reach those unsure of the changes and those implacably opposed can be exchanged for new audiences: as Livne noted in promoting these changes, 'there IS an appetite for discussing these issues more broadly if we just give people a chance … they wouldn't have come to us if they didn't think it was a good story.' (pers.com.)

4.1 Developing Policy

In compiling this policy, I have worked with Hastings Museum and Art Gallery, a regional museum in East Sussex which maintains one of the largest and most significant Native American collections in Britain, containing a number of objects of considerable historical importance. Hastings makes an ideal environment for this study because its collections are not well known abroad and the museum does not have a dedicated subject specialist curator experienced with Indigenous relations.

The current curatorial team, comprised of dedicated and highly experienced museum professionals, have had no formal training or grounding in how to work with Indigenous visitors or communities in relation to their collections. Despite these limitations, the Hastings staff are nevertheless enthusiastic in wanting to engage with Indigenous communities in relation to the collections they hold. The collections with which they work are also unusual; Museum Director Damian Etherington notes that they were assembled not by 'your archetypal Victorian/ Edwardian collectors, so we're having to grapple with slightly different issues than [other museums] where it was clearly collected by Imperial administrators or military adventurers' (pers. com.), because 'the collections we have weren't acquired in the traditional way in which colonial collections were, with most coming from trade or collecting in the 20th century' (Hastings, 2019). These nuances to the origins of the collections, places a different approach to their curation, working with the legacies and grey areas of colonial trade rather than the more direct oppression of seizure and governmental coercion.

Hastings urgently needs more effective engagement with Indigenous communities represented in their collections, a reality well understood by the curatorial team. The galleries have not been refurbished for several decades, and reflect within their labels and displays out-of-date scholarship which the current team are unable, due to lack of resources and in-house knowledge, to easily replace – there is for example no discussion within the gallery of the issues around colonialism and its history in the museum, which Etherington acknowledges is, for practical reasons, currently 'a step too far for us'. Following an unannounced spot visit to the museum in the summer of 2019, Chris Andersen, Professor of Indigenous Studies at the University of Alberta, reported at interview:

> It's a situation where they have a building which already has a particular footprint, inside and outside. They, I wouldn't say, spent a large amount of resources in their exhibit putting in to reshaping the building to sort of better fit the motif they were going for, so its very much a kind of British school-housey kind of building that they were going to put artefacts into... Its very artefact based, and sort of laid out one thing after another.
>
> You know interestingly, the best part [was the Grey Owl display], even though it annoyed me because Grey Owl was actually stationed about an hour from where I grew up, and in our community some thought of him as 'know it all' asshole ... They did the best job with him, because they actually put him in space and time and so even though I was sort of personally annoyed that that was there ... they did the best job on that contextualising the material artefacts that they had. (Andersen, 2019)

Andersen's point here is that in his opinion the museum does a better job at interpreting, and may be more comfortable with, the legacies of Grey Owl, a British imitator of Plains culture, than the colonially assembled collections in their galleries which speak directly about Native American cultures. Etherington acknowledges this point, emphasising that Hastings 'would welcome a project to improve these galleries – just need to find the funding to bring Indigenous curators/ representatives together and also to make the actual changes' (pers. com.). This section contains policy proposals which provide a guide to support Hastings Museum in better educating their visitors about Native American culture of the past and of today, and an adaptable framework by which other museums with comparable collections may structure their engagement with Indigenous visitors and collections.

To develop this policy collaboratively, a partnership was agreed in 2019 between *Beyond the Spectacle* and Hastings, in which the Hastings curatorial team would work with me and Indigenous partners to draft a policy document which laid out a guide of what was expected of staff and the institution for best practice in cultural engagements with Indigenous communities. The policy document which follows was drafted between the autumn of 2019 and the spring of 2020, drawing on interviews with Hastings museum staff and Native American visitors to museums in Britain and the unannounced site visit to Hastings by Chris Anderson and Prof. David Stirrup of the University of Kent. The development process was one of negotiation in which idealised practice ran into the realities of running a resource-limited regional museum, and drafts of the policy were then circulated to a panel of Indigenous American reviewers working the heritage field, and commented on by academics who had worked on similar schemes in North America, going through several iterations in the process. An adapted version of the policy presented in this section was formally adopted by Hastings Museum and Art Gallery on 7 September 2020.

Interspersed within the policy document which follows, discussion sections consider the conversations which went into shaping the policy and presents case studies from other museums in Britain to illustrate why certain parts of the policy came to be incorporated. It considers language, ethos and practical communication, catering both to museum professionals and Indigenous visitors, and creates a document which, during 2020, began the process of being formally signed into Hastings' Museum governance.

The guidance promotes the following key points

1. Museums must be prepared to listen to Indigenous partners on appropriate storage, display and communication and implement their recommendations.

2. Museums must have a clear process by which Indigenous communities can request and obtain repatriation of contested collections.
3. Museums must devote resources to ethical Indigenous engagement, managed if necessary through working groups.
4. Museums will follow best-practice protocols in managing communications with Indigenous partners and in ensuring that visits are planned in sensitive and ethical ways.
5. Museum staff will apply these lessons more broadly across all interactions with Indigenous collections, displays and research, including educational programming, commercial activities and publicity.

4.2 Indigenous Engagement Policy

4.2.1 Introduction

The Indigenous Engagement Policy sets out the considerations for museums working with Indigenous collections and source communities. This policy introduces a guide for *[Museum name]* to use when working with Indigenous people and collections. This includes, but is not limited to collections projects, storage, research, digital initiatives, commercial activities, major redevelopments, re-displays and exhibitions, significant funding bids and educational programming.

This policy provides a starting point from which members of staff should receive further training to support their work with Indigenous peoples and collections.

4.2.2 Principles

[Museum name] treats Indigenous people and collections with the utmost respect and dignity. We acknowledge that the Museum acquired and continues to hold collections of material culture from Indigenous communities and nations and that this can create an imbalanced relationship between the Museum and those collectives. We acknowledge that items now in the collections may have been acquired in situations of unequal relations of power related to colonial and imperial histories. We also acknowledge our responsibility to provide access to these collections for Indigenous communities and nations and to work with them to support their needs. We acknowledge that the presence of items in museums can be traumatic for Indigenous visitors to encounter because of the difficult histories attached to them, and wish to support Indigenous visitors during engagements with them.

[*Museum name*] acknowledges the UN Declaration on the Rights of Indigenous Peoples, to which the United Kingdom is a signatory, and this policy engages with Articles 11 and 12 of that Declaration:

Article 11

1. Indigenous peoples have the right to practise and revitalize their cultural traditions and customs. This includes the right to maintain, protect and develop the past, present and future manifestations of their cultures, such as archaeological and historical sites, artefacts, designs, ceremonies, technologies and visual and performing arts and literature.

2. States shall provide redress through effective mechanisms, which may include restitution, developed in conjunction with indigenous peoples, with respect to their cultural, intellectual, religious and spiritual property taken without their free, prior and informed consent or in violation of their laws, traditions and customs.

Article 12

1. Indigenous peoples have the right to manifest, practise, develop and teach their spiritual and religious traditions, customs and ceremonies; the right to maintain, protect, and have access in privacy to their religious and cultural sites; the right to the use and control of their ceremonial objects; and the right to the repatriation of their human remains.

2. States shall seek to enable the access and/or repatriation of ceremonial objects and human remains in their possession through fair, transparent and effective mechanisms developed in conjunction with indigenous peoples concerned.

Discussion

Taylor Norman has written that 'institutions must be willing and committed to share our side, to show that we are still here, and to confront their own histories as tools of empire. Until this occurs, we will continue to see new presentations … perpetuate woefully outdated discussion' (Norman, 2019i:21). It is this acknowledgement and understanding, not just of Indigenous identity and agency, but of the harm collections can cause, which underpins the need for policy which recognises Indigenous peoples and affirms their rights.

The UN declaration and definition are useful tools in this process, acknowledging that there are groups of peoples left distinct and disadvantaged by historical and contemporary movements of colonialism, and whose cultures are still under threat of harm from this disadvantage. Museums in Britain have often played a part, both individually and as a sector, in perpetuating this harm, such as through acquisition of objects removed unethically from Indigenous communities, or though presentation of Indigenous societies in ways which deny agency to members of those societies and exacerbate harm.

This document recognises that museum staff and educators do not set out to cause harm, but often still do so through a lack of education or resources. It recognises that museum staff are as a body conscientious and eager to engage ethically and meaningfully, but simply do not have the tools to hand, and seeks to provide at least some of those tools to begin to mitigate the errors of the past.

4.2.3 Definitions

Indigenous Peoples

This museum recognises the UN Definition of Indigenous Peoples (2004)[7] :

> Indigenous communities, peoples and nations are those which, having a historical continuity with pre-invasion and pre-colonial societies that developed on their territories, consider themselves distinct from other sectors of the societies now prevailing on those territories, or parts of them. They form at present non-dominant sectors of society and are determined to preserve, develop and transmit to future generations their ancestral territories, and their ethnic identity, as the basis of their continued existence as peoples, in accordance with their own cultural patterns, social institutions and legal system.
>
> This historical continuity may consist of the continuation, for an extended period reaching into the present of one or more of the following factors:
>
> a) Occupation of ancestral lands, or at least of part of them;
> b) Common ancestry with the original occupants of these lands;
> c) Culture in general, or in specific manifestations (such as religion, living under a tribal system, membership of an indigenous community, dress, means of livelihood, lifestyle, etc.);
> d) Language (whether used as the only language, as mother-tongue, as the habitual means of communication at home or in the family, or as the main, preferred, habitual, general or normal language);
> e) Residence on certain parts of the country, or in certain regions of the world;
> f) Other relevant factors.
>
> On an individual basis, an indigenous person is one who belongs to these indigenous populations through self-identification as indigenous (group consciousness) and is recognized and accepted by these populations as one of its members (acceptance by the group).

---

[7] United Nations Permanent Forum on Indigenous Issues, 'Indigenous Peoples, Indigenous Voices – Factsheet', www.un.org/esa/socdev/unpfii/documents/5session_factsheet1.pdf.

The Museum acknowledges that Indigenous collections were obtained from living peoples, and that descendants of these communities still exist today for whom the objects have meaning. These collections include material recovered from archaeological contexts.

Knowledge and Authority

[Museum name] recognises that its staff expertise is limited regarding Indigenous collections. We seek to increase our understanding of these materials by working with members of communities of origin as well as with specialist scholars.

[Museum name] aspires to create an internal working group tasked with developing a plan, as funding and resource permit, to identify or confirm identifications of Indigenous items in the collection. Where possible this will take place through collaboration with wider networks of museum and community experts, as a starting point for notifying communities of origin about the collections the museum holds.

The working group will meet at regular intervals to consider external funding options, discuss project possibilities and communicate with experts to offer preliminary identification of collections by region, culture and community, and to begin to link historic collections to contemporary communities. A key responsibility will be to obtain external funding support for consultation projects with community members in order to facilitate community access, develop educational programming, correct misinformation and ensure best interpretation and care of collections. The working group will aspire to keep up to date with current events and heritage initiatives in the communities from which their collections originate.

[Museum name] staff are aware that Indigenous community members may have differing understandings of and views on heritage/cultural items in the collections and the Museum will commit to incorporating these views into staff practice moving forwards. Staff will, with permission, record Indigenous views of the collections in the museum archives, under the understanding that such records are publicly accessible and that all sources of information are named as transparent practices of good scholarship around collections.

Where we are aware or are informed that objects have cultural or ceremonial significance, or problematic acquisition histories that makes their display or use potentially harmful to Indigenous visitors or communities, the Museum will refrain from publicly displaying these items without adequate consultation and permission from the communities involved, and if displayed, with full contextualisation.

Where we have reason to believe that items in the collection are modern fakes – objects made by non-Indigenous people as imitations of Indigenous material culture – we will document our reasons for this in museum records and refrain from displaying these materials without full contextualisation. We acknowledge that display of faked material can be offensive to Indigenous visitors, and we will signal clearly in all documentation that items are in fact non-Indigenous replicas. We would exhibit such items only in ways which acknowledge their problematic status and address Indigenous concerns about their provenance, and seek advice from Indigenous collaborators as to the most appropriate way to proceed with such objects.

Discussion

It is often hard for museums, relying on incomplete and inaccurate provenance information, to know precisely where collections originate and whom to contact. This was raised in the feedback to early policy drafts, which noted that in collections 'many, many items are listed as 'America', or NWC, which does not enable staff to contact anyone!' However researching and correcting these historic errors is a time-consuming process that requires specialist knowledge.

This is problematic, as feedback noted: 'small museums do not have the staff time or expertise to do this. This requires national-level support... [museums are] willing, but not trained and don't have staff resources.' This was a problem raised in relation to the Haida delegation of 2009, Cara Krmpotich and Laura Peers noting the 'special projects such as the Haida Project tend to draw heavily on staff resources, "hijacking" museum departments ... Museums don't always see the importance of dedicating large amounts of staff time to serving source community needs ... after the special project is over' (Krmpotich and Peers 2013:255).

Working groups are a solution which enables this resource cost to be ring-fenced within specific projects and roles, enabling long-term planning, the development of connections with external specialists and the space to prepare funding applications sustainably. This limits the impact of the Indigenous Access Policy on the museum's limited resources while still demonstrating commitment to the communication process and providing a framework for personnel to facilitate external requests and projects as they arise.

One responsibility of the working group, identified by an Indigenous reviewer, is to keep up to date with current events and heritage initiatives in the communities from which their collections originate. They wrote:

[there should be] policy for the Indigenous collections managers to remain abreast of the current affairs pertaining to the communities they display/ interact with. This is not only good practice for furthering contextual knowledge of the objects held . . . in this way institutions can act as allies, but can also be more adept at interacting with communities whose first priority may not be dealing with objects in a foreign museum.

This process should involve digital tools such as online subscriptions to local news sources, google alerts and social media, as well as direct communication with community organisations.

4.2.4 Repatriation and Retention

[Museum name] holds collections from Indigenous communities for display, research and educational purposes. The Museum presents a clear rationale for how it uses collections and will provide a clear statement on request as to why and how these collections are being used or stored. The Museum will provide an honest, clear and realistic intention of future usage of these collections, and ensure that, as far as is possible, access and engagement with the collections are not impeded when not on public display.

It may be that an Indigenous community will request that objects be repatriated. In this circumstance, *[Museum name]*'s working group will discuss the repatriation of requested parts of the collections back to their source communities. This will be a long-term negotiated process, through which decisions concerning the formal transfer of objects from the collection to communities will take place.

All relevant staff should be aware of the Indigenous Repatriation Handbook, compiled by Indigenous Canadian curators and the Royal British Columbia Museum, and be fully conversant with the issues it raises and the best practice it recommends. It is available for download at https://royalbcmuseum.bc.ca/sites/ default/files/indigenous_repatriation_handbook_rbcm_2019.pdf

Other useful guides, mentioned in Section 1, can be found via the School of Advanced Research, Santa Fe: https://guidelinesforcollaboration.info;and the Smithsonian Center for Folklife and Cultural Heritage: https://folklife-media.si.edu/docs/folklife/Shared-Stewardship.pdf.

Should *[Museum name]* receive a repatriation request from a community or authorised intermediary, the working group should set out to establish the following information:

• A full history of the object(s) in question, including the circumstances of acquisition and its use within the museum since acquisition.

- An understanding of the importance of the object to the community making the repatriation request.
- A designated person or institution, appropriate to act as receiver of the requested object(s).

This process can be time-consuming and require significant staff engagement. The working group should establish and communicate a realistic timescale for this process, outlining clearly the stages required to the requester. Where required, the working group should identify external consultants qualified to review the claim, and prepare budgets and funding applications for the costs involved.

A report will be prepared outlining the findings of this research programme to be circulated to museum stakeholders and the makers of the repatriation request. This will outline clearly the contributory factors involved in deciding whether to proceed with the repatriation, and make a recommendation.

It is crucial that all outstanding claims on object(s) are settled before a decision is made. Communities who may have alternative claims should be consulted, and the process paused until all communities with a claim have reached an agreement on which of them should be the recipient of the object(s) in question. Any conditions which form part of this process on either side, such as photography or scientific study, will be agreed in writing at this stage.

Once a designated recipient has been determined, the claim will be assessed by senior museum management and the museum's governance body for approval. Decisions as to repatriation will be taken on a case-by-case basis, with the presumption that human ancestral remains, sacred or privileged artefacts, and acquisitions made under circumstances which would today be illegal will be prioritised for repatriation to their communities of origin.

The future use or care of object(s) by communities after repatriation will not be a factor in this decision-making process, neither will it be contingent on any payment or payment-in-kind by the Indigenous community.

If the claim is not approved, the report and a detailed explanation of the decision will be supplied to the requestor, with the right of appeal. If the claim is approved, the working group will supply the report and all relevant documentation to its governing body, processing the repatriation claim in accordance with ethical deaccession policy, as described by the Museums Association (www.museumsassociation.org/download?id=11113).

The governing body will, based on the recommendation of the working group, ratify the decision of the senior museum management, or if they do not ratify, will present clear reasons why they have refused, with an invitation to resubmit once concerns have been addressed.

[Museum name] Indigenous working group will take responsibility for packing the object(s) for repatriation, as well as obtaining British export licences. Agreement on responsibility for any fees resulting will form part of the repatriation agreement, with the understanding that external funding may have to be obtained as part of the process. *[Museum name]* will also take responsibility for facilitating any ceremonial activities surrounding the repatriation, as required by Indigenous partners.

All correspondence, reports and other documentation pertaining to the repatriation will remain on file at the Museum for future reference, to establish process and authority over repatriation, should competing claims emerge in the future. Should a case arise in which Indigenous objects are no longer considered part of the Museum's core collections, and are deemed for whatever reason unsuitable for return to source communities (for example, if provenance cannot be established or the community does not want them returned), then *[Museum name]* will follow Museums Association guidelines on ethical disposal in accordance with *[Museum name]*'s Collection Development and Disposals policies.

Discussion

In 2019, Bristol Museum repatriated two ancestors and associated grave materials to the Tongva people of Southern California. These remains had been excavated from a gravesite on Santa Catalina Island in ancestral Tongva territory by amateur archaeologist Alfred Hutchins in the late nineteenth century under circumstances which were at the time legal, but would not be so today.

The process of repatriation, which broadly followed the policy outlined here, took twelve years, and was initiated by a local filmmaker Teri Brewer, who began researching human remains in the Bristol Museum for a documentary in the late 2000s. Working with museum staff and Indigenous Californian community groups, Brewer was able open lines of communication which led to the production of a research report, which contributed to Brewer's 2015 film *A Donation to the Museum*. The following year, after internal Tongva discussions about appropriate recipients, a repatriation request was received by Bristol Museum from the Ti'at Society, a Tongva cultural heritage group.

Processed by the Bristol Museum team through their established disposal process, and with the UCLA Fowler Museum acting as intermediaries on behalf of the Ti'at Society, the repatriation request was accepted and recommended by museum director Jon Finch and approved by first Bristol City Council and then

Mayor Marvin Rees. At a ceremony in Bristol City Hall on 28 March 2019, the ancestors were returned to a Tongva delegation. In her speech accepting the ancestors, curator Desiree Martinez stated, 'We are grateful that the Bristol City Museum and Gallery has been gracious enough to work with us to make this possible' (Postans, 2019).

What Bristol's experience demonstrates is that by managing a process along clear disposal and repatriation guidelines, maintaining open communication and understanding Indigenous priorities in the repatriation process, repatriations can be achieved without conflict, building strong relationships for better collaborative curation.

4.2.5 Cultural Sensitivity

[Museum name] is aware that its collections may contain items which are deemed sensitive, gendered, animate or secret/sacred to Indigenous peoples. We will strive to learn more about these issues as we work with members of Indigenous communities, and add any information received to the Museum's records about specific items and their appropriate treatment.

We will endeavour to catalogue and describe all Indigenous collections clearly to provide warnings when items are deemed to be culturally sensitive by Indigenous communities. This will enable people to avoid encountering the object or photographs of it should they not wish to see it. This consideration particularly applies to human remains, material thought to have been removed from burial sites and objects with religious or spiritual power.

The Museum will make every effort to store, conserve, interpret and display collections in accordance with the cultural protocols of the source communities. We will seek guidance on culturally appropriate collections care issues from Indigenous consultants and in collaboration with specialist researchers and organisations, such as the Museum Ethnographers Group, who can share knowledge from Indigenous co-researchers.

The Museum will make decisions regarding display, storage and access of collections on a case-by-case basis on objects that have cultural restrictions placed on them by source communities, based on advice from those communities. It will consider the feasibility, legal implications and health and safety regulations when making these decisions. Once decisions have been made *[Museum name]* will make all parties, staff and Indigenous communities aware of the reasons for choosing the action it takes. This information will be added to the collections management system and also the object files.

Discussion

During a visit to the British Museum, Aquinnah Wampanoag weaver Linda Coombes was horrified when a conservator suggested repairing a wampum belt with loose beads.

> There was one belt that had, it looked like a row was coming loose and there was one bead hanging down like it was the start of the next row going back up, and it looked like some beads had been lost at whatever point in time. And I was actually surprised by the conservator's question: should that be fixed, repaired? And for everything I've learned in my career is that you don't repair an artefact, but that you stabilise it in the condition in which it is in ... I thought that was odd. And particularly on a wampum belt. It is not the place of a museum conservator to do anything like fix it. You just don't, you know? (Coombes, 2019)

Though Wampum is a type of object with strong social and ceremonial importance to the Wampanoag, Coombes makes it clear that she applies this irritation about this type of unsolicited intervention across the whole material collections: for Coombes, experienced in Wampanoag museum practices, unwarranted interventions such as the conservator proposed were wholly inappropriate.

One way to address some of these issues is through acknowledgements, not just of specific harm or potential for harm, but of general sector-wide problems. Jenny Marlowe has identified how this works in another sector, suggesting that the route to better communication can lie in formally identifying that harm in approachable ways. At interview, she highlighted an example of an acknowledgement she worked on at an arts organisation in Los Angeles which not only acknowledged the indigenous owners of the land they were on, but the harm that the principle arts industries of that city have caused:

> [The key to] this land acknowledgment was that we didn't just write that we live and work on Tongva, Tataviam and Chumash land. It also talked about the culpability of Hollywood, being in L.A. . . . . [W]e felt that it was really important to acknowledge that the place that we all live and work bears a lot of responsibility for the negative images of Native people that we see all around us, and to talk about that. So it grappled with our own environment, our neighbourhood and our city's responsibility for some of the bad things that happened around representation of Native people. The stereotyping . . . Hollywood as an industry bears a lot of responsibility for that, and as an arts association in Los Angeles, we were tied to benefiting from our association with that industry, so we felt that it was important to acknowledge.' (Marlowe, 2020)

Museums can learn from this – it isn't enough to acknowledge specific harms, but to start conversations about more general harms caused by this vast object archive held thousands of miles away from its origin, so that all that follows is accurately contextualised within that framework.

4.2.6 Governance

We recognise the importance of including Indigenous peoples in the care of Indigenous heritage items. As part of our plan to improve the care of Indigenous collections, we aspire to locate and build relationships with appropriate Indigenous advisors who can participate in meetings and provide guidance on a regular basis. We will build appropriate budget lines into future planning, research, storage and gallery projects to include advisors for particular Indigenous collections to advise the Museum on future care and display of these collections, including honoraria for advisors and appropriate travel funding. We will minute, archive and implement Indigenous advisors' advice as far as possible given resource limitations. We will communicate Indigenous advisors' guidance to the museum's governing stakeholders, and when appropriate, we will consider appointing Indigenous collaborators to governing bodies.

4.2.7 Guidance

The following sections each provided detailed guidance on how *[Museum name]* will appropriately handle engagement with Indigenous collections and the peoples from whom they came originally.

Opening Communications with Indigenous Communities

Indigenous communities have the right to know where their material culture is kept in collections. The Museum acknowledges its responsibility to ensure collections are accurately identified and to maintain contact with communities of origin, as resource permits.

Once communities of origin are confirmed by the working group listed in Section 3, the Museum will, as resource permits:

- Aspire to proactively contact tribal cultural centres or heritage officers where possible to inform them that *[Museum name]* may hold collections from their communities.
- Provide these correspondents a list of the objects within the collection, with images where possible, and include any information known about their circumstances of transfer to the Museum (including collector name).
- Ensure that the Indigenous community understands that they are welcome to nominate representatives to give advice to the working group on appropriate

storage, display and interpretation of the objects, and to inform Museum staff how the Museum can most productively work with community members to support community access.

The working group is aware that heritage officers, NAGPRA officers, cultural centres and other community contacts change over time, and will aspire to maintain contacts and if necessary locate other appropriate community advisors if initial contacts fail to respond. The Museum recognises that many Indigenous people live outside Indigenous communities, and aspires as resource permits to make images and information about the collections available publicly, where possible online.

When engaging in dialogue with Indigenous people *[Museum name]* will aspire to:

- Make every effort to fulfil requests for images and information in a timely manner.
- Keep Indigenous correspondents honestly informed of resources and time-scales, alterations based on their advice and limitations of what is possible.
- Ask Indigenous contributors if it is appropriate to record information and where that is the case, permanently archive, as far as is compliant with data-protection and GDPR laws, all communications with Indigenous communities or correspondents.
- Remember that community partners are often working voluntarily, and do not impose deadlines or conditions upon them, allowing them to define the pace of progression on any collaboration.
- Ensure that any professional work undertaken by Indigenous partners at the museum's behest is compensated appropriately, at industry rates.

Discussion

The question of from where collaboration should spring, and whether responsibility for initiating contact lies with the museum or the community from which the objects come, is complex because it requires expertise on both sides which may be lacking. Principally lacking is the knowledge from communities as to which institutions hold material culture from their community, and within the museum as to where precisely their collections came from and whom within those communities it is appropriate for them to work with. Eleanor Lanyon of Hastings expressed this concern at interview: 'How would anyone know what we've got, and how would we go about finding the people who wanted to engage with the collection?' (Hastings, 2019).

Taylor Norman articulated at interview that this lack of knowledge shouldn't preclude museums making that first step:

> I think that the openness and the initial reach out to communities has to come from museums ... I feel like the responsibility lies with them to engage and say, we know this has been put out there, let me reach out, right? Because we have a lot of problems at home beyond museums in other countries. I mean, tribal leadership are swamped, elders have a lot that they have to deal with and the youth, we are trying to do everything all at once, so it's a lot to try and keep tabs on ... [I]t has to be on the people handling that specific collection to reach out, and try to go through the right channels ... to do things in a good way. (Norman, 2019ii)

Linda Coombes, the Wampanoag weaver who came to Britain in search of Wampum belts, agreed, but noted that once contact had begun, the museums should let the Indigenous community lead the process:

> In my mind the belts belong to us, to the Native people, so we should lead the conversation, and I think the British should listen and then we go from there ... To me, it is like, duh! Whose stuff did it come from? What people did this stuff come from that is now being dug out of the ground? They own it. And who'sever doing the archaeology or whatever scientific process, they need to go to those people. And then [they say] 'well those people don't exist anymore!' Then find their cousins, because they're out there somewhere. (Coombes, 2019)

Coombes' point is supported by feedback on the initial draft policy, which identified this as an area of potential conflict, even exploitation, if not carefully managed, noting that 'if every museum is doing this then there should be funding for consultants at a national level to work out priorities. You cannot ask Indigenous people to consult for free and you need to work out who is best to advise without having 30 museums all ask the same person to ID their collections.' The solution to this problem seems to be museums notifying community organisations of the existence of their material culture in the museum's collection, but then allowing those community organisations to decide whether and to what extent they wish to work with the museum on their own timetable in accordance with their own goals and resources.

Norman summarised this problem in the conclusion to her own work:

> It is fundamental to emphasize that Native voice is not meant to be a static fixture with exhibits as a quote or recording. Native voice is critique. Native voice is presence. Native voice is collaboration. To engage in meaningful dialogue with our communities beyond what is necessary for initial research steps in creating must be taken to create space with ambitions beyond colonial museological paradigms. (Norman, 2019i:35)

Digital Access to Collections by Indigenous Peoples

[Museum name] will endeavour where possible to make Indigenous collections accessible via the internet. The Museum aspires to include the following information where possible:

- Digital images of the objects. These can include but are not limited to low and high resolution images, survey images of the reverse, underside, inside, and construction/decoration details.
- Place of collection.
- Date of collection.
- Who it was collected by.
- A clearly defined process by which Indigenous correspondents can provide feedback on records, through correspondence with the museum.

Where possible, materials connected to living and identifiable descendants should be prioritised for digitisations of Indigenous collections.

The Museum acknowledges advantages to participating in digital portals such as GRASAC and UBC's Reciprocal Research Network in order to provide greatest digital access for Indigenous peoples. The working group will explore opportunities to collaborate with these networks, and aspires to participate in principle, with the understanding that external funding and resources will likely be required to implement such participation.

Discussion

Digital engagement is increasingly cited as the next frontier of museum participation, but for many museums digital infrastructure is too primitive to allow for any but the most basic interaction. Hastings Museum, for instance, currently has no online object database and its online presence for the substantial Native collections is limited to a digital highlights gallery. Other museums with large collections do have searchable databases, but they are rarely designed with Indigenous sensibilities or priorities in mind and can lead to unfortunate encounters.

Taylor Norman expressed her dissatisfaction with the process at interview:

> Well I had a very difficult time with the British Museum's collection. Even finding the Creek stuff, I put in all of our different names, all of the different spellings you could do of Mvskoke and Mvskoke (Creek) and just Creek and each different one came up with different results, and so I would say the British Museum's is very difficult. The Horniman's is a little bit easier but I did not have the best time with that as when I was going through the collections for the

Americas I found a mummified toddler that was in the collections and it was completely [pause].... it was completely uncovered and just sitting there and I was like 'this is supposed to be a children's museum!' ... for me its not [pause] there's no respect in that.

She went on to note approvingly of an American project 'which allows museums and collections to work with tribes to put stickers and labels and a codified label system on who can access different objects' (Norman, 2019ii).

The issue of resolution is one which requires a multilayered solution. Some recent projects with African collections have sought to focus on providing lower-resolution images which are easier to download for those is low-bandwidth internet connections. However in draft feedback for this policy, it was noted that 'a single "coffee table" overall image does not suffice for Indigenous makers', who will require much more detail in order to reproduce techniques and designs remotely.

When planning digitisation projects, museums should therefore liaise with Indigenous partners on their requirements and factor multiple audiences and their diverse technological infrastructure into their provision. In all such provision it is critical that there is a clear system in place by which researchers, Indigenous and otherwise, can communicate with the museum on improving records and obtaining additional images.

Physical Access to Collections by Indigenous Visitors

We acknowledge that Indigenous researchers may have personal and cultural requirements for their engagement with collection items, and we will support these to the best of our ability.

When planning visits by Indigenous peoples to visit *[Museum name]* will:

- Explain in the first instance the nature of the collections which are available.
- Provide a range of dates on which the collections can be accessed.
- Provide details of the physical and environmental nature of the space in which the encounter will take place.
- Provide details of any regulations attached to the visit and discuss normal museum protocol for working with researchers (e.g. visits are normally invigilated by staff; staff work with visitors to determine the limits of handling for especially fragile items; what happens with gifts and offerings; how smudging – the burning of sweetgrass as a blessing – or water cleansing are normally managed).
- Ask Indigenous visitors for any specific requirements they may have – these may include but may not be limited to a desire for privacy while working with

collections, prayer, ceremony (including making offerings and smudging or cleansing with water) or performance in honour of the objects, a desire for handling or wearing of objects in question.

- Be open to serious discussion of issues such as authority over collections and repatriation, with reference to existing established policy and processes, and including key stakeholders.
- *[Museum name]* will try to facilitate access to as many objects as possible during visits by Indigenous groups. However, it will be honest about the restrictions with Indigenous visitors, and will agree to a list of objects to be viewed during the visit in advance to limit any disappointment.
- Agree who from the museum staff will be present during the meeting.
- Ask for a list of the Indigenous groups delegation members.
- Agree to photography permissions for taking photographs of the visit by the museum for any use including for publicity or publications.
- Make visitors aware of local refreshment options, agreeing to catering and dietary requirements where possible.
- Offer the opportunity for the delegation to deliver engagement activities and/ or staff training as part of their visit to the museum's visitors, but do not expect these services to be provided without compensation.
- Follow up requests for further information made during the visit in a timely manner.

When supporting Indigenous visitors access to the collections on site, *[Museum name]* staff will:

- Approach these interactions with an open mind and in a respectful manner.
- Acknowledge that the encounter may be deeply emotional and even distressing for Indigenous visitors, as well as inspiring, and seek to support visitors.
- Verbally reconfirm permission for taking of photographs during the visit and discuss how images might be used by the museum. All photographs taken will be made available to the delegation for use without reservation or restrictions. Any museum uses of images should be reconfirmed for each use (e.g. social media, annual report, grant applications). Staff members also have the right to refuse to appear in photographs.
- Offer opportunities for educational programming or public speaking should visitors wish to engage with the public, and be open to discussion of commercial opportunities for visitors within the museum's commercial spaces.

Discussion

Physical access to collections is a critical component of any relationship between an Indigenous community and a museum. No photograph, video, replica or 3D rendering could ever recapitulate the significance of direct engagement with historic objects. Though the geographical, financial and logistical barriers are significant, Indigenous delegations to museums are a regular feature of curatorial practice and must be managed sensitively and effectively.

In 2011, a delegation from the Inuinnait visited the British Museum, sponsored by the Northwest Territories Literacy Council for a documentary on the CBC. An account of the visit noted:

> We watch as the Inuinnait interact with the clothing and tools, figuring out what they were for and how they were made. We see them laughing, as they remember stories and songs; we cry with them as they realize these objects are the embodiment of their ancestors. We hear them wondering what the last songs were that a 100-year old drum heard. We hear them marvelling at how well the objects are made. We watch and listen as they try to remember 'sleeping words'. (NWT Literacy Council, 2016)

Every museum with collections obtained from Indigenous peoples must have a plan for staff to follow to ensure that this kind of interaction is possible, safe and fulfilling for visitors and exercised with maximum respect for Indigenous protocol.

Facilitating Ceremonies by Indigenous Visitors

Ceremonies in relation to object collections are common, and range from prayers in Indigenous languages through dances honouring historic ancestors, burning of food stuffs or other materials and smudging ceremonies. *[Museum name]* will honour requests from Indigenous peoples for ceremonies as far as possible by:

- Providing clear guidance for visitors on accessibility and capability via the museum's website.
- Providing honest communication in the initial stages of the visit to allow for respectful negotiation on these issues in advance.
- Working with Indigenous researchers to understand what kind of space is needed and with colleagues to provide suitable spaces for ceremonies within the building, the Museum grounds, or identifying and securing appropriate permissions for suitable alternative nearby locations for the ceremonies (e.g. public parks).

- Clarifying in advance whether the ceremony is public or private. If public, then the museum should make patrons aware that it is to take place, the serious nature of the event and the importance of respectful observation.
- Clarifying in advance whether museum staff are welcome to participate or to witness and what is not appropriate for staff to do.
- Determining whether smoke detectors can be turned off for ceremonies involving smoke, and if not, explain to Indigenous visitors and offer outdoor spaces. Ceremonial participants may be asked to work with staff to facilitate such ceremonies indoors by limiting the amount of material burned so as not to set off smoke detectors; fire personnel may be appropriately involved as witnesses; or staff may choose to move collections outdoors so they can be smudged.
- Agreeing upon a timetable and including time for quiet reflection after the ceremony.

The space in which an interaction between Indigenous peoples and collections takes place should be prepared in advance of the visit. *[Museum name]* will make sure that:

- The room is uncluttered and with space for the visitors to move about. Care should be taken that there are no materials in the room which might cause offence. Where a choice of rooms is possible, the room should be situated so that inappropriate environmental conditions, such as excessive noise, do not intrude.
- Suitable lighting is provided if there is limited or no natural light.
- The room is accessible for all visitors; Indigenous groups often include elders who may have mobility difficulties.
- Only staff essential to the visit and approved in advance are in the room.

Discussion

Ceremony is very important for visiting Indigenous groups, helping to mitigate the harm of the museum environment while also connecting the Indigenous participants more closely with the material heritage and the ancestors to whom they are connected by these collections. These ceremonies often require specific activities and environments for which museums are not well designed. A curator wrote in policy feedback, 'A lot of ceremony needs to happen outdoors. Museums could think about where they might access a fairly private outdoor space – this has been the greatest challenge in my experience!'

In 2012, a delegation from the Siksika Blackfoot people visited the British Museum. Unfamiliar with the procedures that Museum requires, they gave less than 48-hours notice of their visit to Museum staff who, given the importance of the visiting delegation, made an exception to the usual rules and worked overtime to ensure that the delegates would have the opportunity to view the Blackfoot collections.

However, the short notice meant that there was no time for museum staff to prepare for any ceremonial activities the delegates wished to conduct. Thus, when the delegates requested the opportunity to conduct a smudging prayer over the collections, there had been no clearance arranged with the security teams to permit the use of smoke in collection spaces. The only available outdoor space was a car park area filled with skips, refrigeration units and staff cars.

The sacred ceremony, so important to the visit for the Siksika, took place amid this inappropriate setting, a result which hopefully did not lessen the value of the ceremony, but was hardly ideal in mitigating the potential for harm that exists within the museum environment. Better advance communication, and a pre-prepared staff plan designating a location and internal protocol for such ceremonies would have prevented this problem from occurring.

Staff Briefing and Approach

The Museum will nominate a manager to coordinate the visit, who will:

- Ensure staff interacting directly with supporting Indigenous visitors are aware of supporting material to fulfil the encounter in a respectful manner and support collaborative engagement.
- Make all museum staff aware, whether or not they are specifically involved in coordinating the visit, that Indigenous people will be visiting the museum and ensure that visitors receive a warm welcome. Respectful protocol for engaging with visitors, including modes of address, should be established in advance and circulated to all staff, and where staff are aware that Indigenous engagements with collection items may require specific ceremonies, all colleagues should be briefed on what to expect and how to behave.
- All staff and volunteers directly facilitating the visit should be briefed regarding the nature/cultural affiliation(s) of the visitors, the nature of the collections to be worked with, the agreed timetable, and any known requirements on space and noise and any potential disruption to the museum's standard operations.
- Ensure that the visit is integrated with the museum's environment. For example, quiet contemplative visits or engagements with ancestral remains/

sensitive materials should not be disturbed by noisy school groups or routine maintenance. Visitor services/front of house staff should also be supported in any potentially emotionally charged conversations with visitors or ceremonial activity in the public areas of the museum.

- Museum staff must recognise that Indigenous visitors can come to the museum as learners rather than as experts, and that even Indigenous visitors who know about items may not wish or be able to comment on them. Terms under which information is shared should be agreed in advance, and staff should refrain from directly questioning Indigenous visitors during the visit about the collections they are working with outside these agreements. After a visit, it may be appropriate for staff to ask if the visitor has information they wish the Museum to add to the records, making it clear that such records are publicly available and online. Information volunteered by the Indigenous visitors should be recorded and placed directly into the catalogue records for the object in question with permission and full attribution.

Discussion

During the preparations for the major Haida delegation to the Pitt-Rivers Museum in 2009 documented in the book *This Is Our Life*, curator Laura Peers worked with Haida counterparts to develop a document entitled 'Staff Notes for Haida Visit'. Circulated to all staff, including those in roles unlikely to interact directly with the Haida such as maintenance and cleaning, it explained in accessible language why the Haida were visiting the museum, why the visit was so significant for the Haida and for the Museum, and gave key dates and personnel. It included a cheery recommendation that staff should 'Please introduce yourself, help them feel welcome at the museum, and provide assistance where required.'

This document meant that anybody who worked in the museum, whether involved in this visit or not, could be prepared should they meet members of the delegation to react appropriately, including cleaners, maintenance and office staff who lack the specialist training and experience of the curatorial team. It allowed these staff to plan their own activities around the delegation, avoiding, for example, using noisy equipment during sessions, while educating them on the importance of the visit and their role in making it successful.

A copy of the document, preserved in the Pitt-Rivers Museum archives is presented in this Element in the Appendix.

Handling

In order to facilitate culturally appropriate forms of engagement with historic collections, and reconnection with items long held away from communities, *[Museum name]* will endeavour to support handling access to Indigenous collections during visits – even if this goes against normal procedures and practice. Handling will only not be permitted when the collections pose a risk to health or are too fragile to be touched, and this will be clearly explained to visitors in such cases. Where possible staff should work across departments (conservation, curatorial, technical services) to support handling and use.

[Museum name] will ensure standard collections care assessment practices are followed when assessing the suitability of collections for handling during these visits. Where it is not possible to touch the collections, this will be communicated in advance to the delegation and full and proper reasons given for this decision.

The museum will aspire to ensure that requests for more elaborate forms of contact with collections are met where possible. These may include requests to wear clothing or even to dance in it, to play musical implements or to experiment with weapons and equipment handling. These should be considered on a case-by-case basis, and where harm to the object and visitor can be minimised and where doing so would have a significant beneficial effect for the visitor it should be permitted.

Staff are encouraged to work with Indigenous visitors to seek creative solutions in order to support Indigenous engagements. Staff should not view physical alterations to items as a result of handling as damage to the object, but as marks of the item's ongoing biography and interaction with the Indigenous communities from which it came.

Discussion

In preparation for the 2009 Haida delegation to the Pitt-Rivers Museum, Laura Peers and Kate Jackson noted that 'handling of collections by research visitors goes beyond that which is normally permitted by museums, and thus the request had to be discussed and assessed by staff ... These behind the scenes discussions have significant bearing on the level of engagement source communities can have with museum collections' (Krmpotich & Peers, 2013:59). The focus of these discussions was on musical instruments, Haida musicians being permitted to use their own informed judgement on playing flutes and rattles.

However an unanticipated handing encounter came on the first day, when the group viewed a collection of fish clubs. Two of the group snatched up clubs and began to strike at one another. The delegates were simply recreating the physicality of the original owners of the objects, using them as the Haida understand they should be used. To the museum staff though, who stepped in to break up the mock battle, this sort of unplanned interaction risked putting the objects in danger of damage.

These are the kind of decisions that museum staff have to face when Indigenous source communities come into contact with historic collections repurposed in the museum space. They will not always be the interactions staff have anticipated or for which they are prepared, and judgements have to be made on what is possible in the circumstances. Using established, published guidance to manage such spontaneous interactions is critical in preventing damage and disappointment and promoting positive engagement.

Privacy

[Museum name] will honour requests for Indigenous visitors to spend time alone with the objects.

Where it is imperative that staff do remain in the room, those staff should make every effort to remain inconspicuous and provide the visitors with privacy in the space. Ensure phones are off or silent, avoid typing or other intrusive activity and do not take photographs unless explicitly invited to do so. Do not interrupt unless safety is imperilled.

Children

[Museum name] welcomes children as part of Indigenous delegations. We recognise the critical opportunities for education and exploration that these experiences offer for children of Indigenous communities. Children will be permitted in the research space and other secure areas of the museum, provided appropriate health and safety and safeguarding procedures are followed.

Photography

[Museum name] will provide existing digital images of collections to Indigenous people for free and without any restrictions on copyright or use. Low- or high-resolution images should be supplied as required and available and accessible. New images should be available for commission at cost.

Catering

For some Indigenous visitors, particularly those who live in very different conditions to Britain, diet can be highly problematic (many Indigenous visitors may be diabetic, lactose-intolerant, etc.). *[Museum name]* will acknowledge any catering and dietary requirements in advance of the visit, and attempt to provide local options for visitors as possible.

Gifts

Gifts are a common part of many Indigenous encounters with museum collections, and are usually reflective of a mutual respect and collaboration. Museum staff should prepare to receive gifts at the end of a visit, and should prepare to reciprocate with an appropriate gift. This could be a guidebook to the museum or local community. Institutional gifts of substantial value should be accessioned into the museum's collection as a respectful legacy of the exchange. Gifts of token value may be kept by staff, based on personal and management discretion.

Discussion

In 2012, a Cherokee group visited Britain to tour the sites visited by the Cherokee delegation of 1762. As the then–Museum Assistant for North America, I helped to facilitate their visit to the British Museum, coordinating between three departments and the visitors to arrange viewing of the materials they wished to see.

At the culmination of the visit, all of the staff who worked with the delegation, including myself, were given pottery vessels by P. J. Gilliam Stewart, a Cherokee artist who produces skeuomorphic jars decorated as if they were woven baskets. Valued at US$30 each, these vessels were under the threshold at which they had to be declared, and were accepted gratefully by the staff who received them.

Refusing these gifts would have been highly insulting to the Cherokee, for whom they were an integral part of the exchange which had taken place. The British Museum did not in this case present visitors with gifts as part of the exchange, but when the *Beyond the Spectacle* project welcomed Native partners for residencies and visiting delegations, we marked their collaboration with the presentation of books relevant to the project, such as Coll Thrush's *Indigenous London*, the gift cementing both the relationship and the collaborative ambitions achieved by coming together.

Collections Care and Management

[Museum name] maintains its collections management and care practice in line with Accreditation and sector best-practice standards.

Documentation

[Museum name] will, where possible, update collections documentation to include Indigenous terminologies and taxonomies. The museum is mindful that traditional categorisations used by museums may be inaccurate and can be offensive to Indigenous visitors, and in such cases staff will endeavour to consult directly on appropriate terminology, replace offensive terms where possible and provide content warnings where not (i.e. historical document archives).

Storage

Access to the collections stores is strictly controlled, to ensure that untrained or unauthorised persons are unable to interact with the collections in ways which might potentially be disrespectful.

Storage of collections adheres to best practice for the sector but can be modified to meet cultural protocols. Indigenous visitors should be granted access to any storage areas housing material culture from their communities, supervised for their safety, to see how materials are stored.

If the museum uses plastic wrap, Tyvek or other forms of non-organic protective covering, particularly if these materials will still be present during a visit to the collection, then the reasons for this should be clearly articulated within the museum's own policy document, explaining the hazards they mitigate, the materials from which they are made, and the methods by which they are attached.

Display and Interpretation

[Museum name] will follow this guide to ensure that all displays which feature Indigenous material culture or history are respectful and appropriate. Many Indigenous visitors will visit *[Museum name]* without prior announcement, and the museum should aspire to ensure that all such visitors are accommodated in the museum space without prior individual arrangement.

Consultancy

For new projects involving Indigenous collections, including redisplay, *[Museum name]* aims to include Indigenous voices in the process. This will be achieved through using Indigenous consultancy determined through collaboration with communities of origin and incorporated into funding applications to support this work where there is no core budget available. Indigenous consultants will be incorporated into the decision-making process via a clear working agreement, and involved in developing the schedule to ensure that community decision-making, via workshops and presentations, is possible.

Feedback should be documented and incorporated whenever possible, and, when it is not, clear rationale for its omission based on time, resource and institutional policy should be given to the Indigenous consultant in writing and preserved for the record.

Key Priorities

[Museum name] accepts that Indigenous priorities within a gallery space are not necessarily the same as British priorities, and these potential competitors must be reconciled as part of the development process.

Key Indigenous priorities to enable this process include:

• Recognition of cultural difference. European-imposed categories rarely apply effectively across Indigenous collections for Indigenous peoples. Indigenous collections come from specific peoples and places, and where known these original owners should be acknowledged in displays, along with Indigenous ways of understanding the objects.

• Recognition of continuity. Although it is common for European collections to have been obtained in the late nineteenth and early twentieth centuries, displays should ensure that they extend beyond this period in depiction – ensure that Indigenous communities are portrayed as living peoples, with evolving traditions, not fixed in time or authenticity due to the shortcomings of collections. Acquire contemporary art where possible, and portray and discuss contemporary Indigenous life.

• Acknowledge in displays the harm which European governance and collecting practices has caused to Indigenous communities, as a first step to mitigating or even starting the healing process.

• Indigenous objects are not art in a classical European sense. Even contemporary Indigenous art does not exist without context, and historic Indigenous art is nothing but context. Focusing on aesthetics to the exclusion of this context primitivises and misappropriates the object.

• Indigenous objects are not curiosities. They have meaning and significance which is often difficult for non-Indigenous audiences to grasp.

• Provide clear information on how visitors can provide feedback on the display, and review feedback regularly. Any feedback from Indigenous visitors will be specifically reviewed by the working group, who will assess the feasibility of affecting changes.

Recognising that Indigenous objects require motion and voice to be properly understood is essential. Work with Indigenous consultancies to incorporate physicality and movement to the displays. Show how objects moved and interacted in their original contexts, for insight into their original roles in Indigenous material culture.

Discussion

As Taylor Norman noted earlier, Indigenous objects themselves have their own agency within institutions, and thus when storage and display of Indigenous collections is planned it is essential that the potential personhood of the objects in the collection is taken into account, and only Indigenous communities are well-placed to interpret these requirements.

Chris Andersen expressed surprise at interview at the realisation that the British Museum did not factor this aspect into the development of their Native American Gallery when it was opened in 1999, and to what degree the display was dictated by the allotted space rather than the other way around:

> I'm not super impressed with the exhibit, or the gallery itself, but I will say that, as you know I spent ten days looking through all of the non-confidential material and the building of it, and what struck me most in the building of that was in relative terms how little discussion was actually put into what material culture would go in, and what would stay out. 90% of the records are basically how do you keep a room between 20 and 21 degrees Celsius . . . from my perspective I was, as a neophyte, I was quite surprised by the manner in which the physical limitations of the building shaped the kinds of things that get produced in a building like that. (Andersen, 2019).

This applies to display as well, ensuring that curators construct displays which educate rather than stereotype – Norman again, critiquing the Plains display at the Horniman museum:

> I observed a family view the display. The father looked at his child and repeatedly hit his hand against his mouth in a mocking gesture to supplement the child's experience. But who could blame him? The faceless mannequin posed with a gun in hand could do nothing to disprove that Plains culture is more than what is portrayed in Hollywood movies. (Norman, 2019i:26)

In these examples, museum staff could have avoided these problems by inviting community consultation and curatorial engagement into these projects at early stages, listening to advice and learning better ways to convey the stories they wanted the objects to tell, as well as acknowledging that their voices are less important in the development of the displays than those of the Indigenous peoples represented.

Educational Programming

[Museum name] provides educational resources to assist visitors, particularly school children, in interpreting the collections, and delivers educational programs to elementary, secondary and HE students. Such materials should be developed based on or in association with Indigenous consultancy, and should operate under the same consideration as the digital and physical gallery space listed in the previous section.

Activities should be respectful of Indigenous sensitivities, and avoid simplifying or objectifying objects or cultures, particularly those held to be sacred or socially reserved. Mimicry, which can be easily interpreted as mockery, such as non-Indigenous staff or visitors performing Indigenous songs or ceremonies, dressing-up or re-enacting exercises, should be avoided entirely unless specifically designed and permitted by an Indigenous partner.

Educational materials should emphasise continuity of Indigenous life, and direct students towards digital resources created by Indigenous people which highlight in particular Indigenous music, dance and other art forms not represented in the gallery space.

All educational material developed by specialist museum educators should be developed jointly by educational and curatorial teams, and double-checked by curatorial teams before publication to ensure errors have not occurred in the editorial process.

[Museum name] welcomes requests from Indigenous visitors to present on some aspect of their culture or art practice to our visitors. The museum will make all possible efforts to facilitate this opportunity, dependent on notice, space and scheduling.

[Museum name] will not edit or censor these engagements, even when the visitor is critiquing or criticising the museum as part of the event. The museum will accept the criticism as constructive advice and try to act to resolve the issues raised.

Commercial Opportunity

If a museum is displaying Indigenous artworks, either historic or contemporary, it is important to recognise that the continued viability of commercial Indigenous art plays a vital role in the continuance of Indigenous artistic traditions.

Museums should therefore offer Indigenous artists from collaborating communities the opportunity to sell products, including but not limited to books, textiles, souvenirs, small-scale mass-produced artworks and large-scale commercial art, in the museum's shop, on terms mutually agreed under contract (such as sale-or-return, or on commission).

Non-Indigenous commercial designers, makers and other artists who wish to access Indigenous collections to develop commercial applications should be referred to appropriate Indigenous communities in the first instance, and only then to speak to the museum. This will ensure that there is no cultural appropriation of collections for commercial gain.

Publicity

[Museum name] should publicise and acknowledge the important Indigenous collections in their galleries through promotional literature and advertisements, but in doing so should follow the guide to ensure that exploitation and stereotyping are avoided and that such materials are sensitive and positive in their portrayal of Indigenous cultures.

Discussion

Museums pursuing marketing strategies involving Indigenous collections must not only act ethically, but be seen to do so.

As an example, the use at Hastings of a Plains war bonnet as the map symbol for visitors to locate their Native American Gallery – by no means a Plains-exclusive space – has been criticised by Chris Andersen following his visit to the museum: 'They have a number racist caricatures in there; they have the little logo over the door [of each gallery] to tell you which one you are going into and its just sort of a fierce looking chief with a headdress' (2019).

Andersen was referring here to the use by the museum, dating back before the present curatorial team was in post, of silhouettes of Plains war bonnets as signposts through the museum directing visitors to the Native American galleries. Chosen as an easy reference point, Andersen's concern is that the use of sacred regalia normally reserved for specific people among specific communities simplifies the audiences' expectation of the museum's Native American museum spaces into caricature, reinforcing negative stereotypes historically perpetrated through Hollywood films and Wild West Shows.

---

5 Conclusion

In this Element I've sought to explore the basis for the problems that arise when Native North American visitors seek to explore their historic material culture in museum spaces and provide both theoretical changes in approach and practical solutions to these problems. Some of the most significant lie in the gulf between intention and impact – museum staff do not intend to offend or perpetuate harm; their intention is to respectfully and educationally display and present these collections to British audiences. However, they too often lack the specialist knowledge required to achieve this without causing the kind of harm described in the opening section.

The goal to improving this situation lies in museum staff acknowledging this lack of knowledge, being transparent about the harm of the past, and working with Indigenous partners to develop displays, interpretation and collection strategies which not only prevent future harm, but can mitigate the historic legacies through honesty and collaboration. This requires museums to be responsive to contemporary Native priorities, including where appropriate, repatriation of objects to their communities of origin.

Museums in Britain hold a vast reservoir of Native American historic material culture, one of the greatest accumulations of Native history anywhere in the world. These collections, and their colonial histories, place on museums an ethical responsibility to be responsive to the calls from Native visitors to represent their histories properly and accurately, to not assume knowledge, but to listen respectfully.

This volume is intended to provide museum staff with the most basic of tools to begin this process and understand what is at stake in their collections and simple steps to follow to begin to participate in 'research as a form of healing', mitigate harm and navigate the crises they face to a more equitable and ethical future.

Appendix

make their living as carvers, weavers, jewellers, commercial fishermen and crabbers, and within natural resource management and the heritage sector.

How are the Haida represented within the Pitt Rivers Museum?

* There are nearly 300 artefacts from Haida Gwaii in the collections at the Museum. Some were collected prior to 1884, while others were collected as recently as 2005. These have been taken off display, or retrieved from storage, in order for the Haida and museum staff to work with them during the visit.
* The central totem pole in the Court is from the Haida village of Old Massett, and once stood in front of Star House which belonged to an Eagle family, the Sea Eggs, a branch of the Stastas lineage.
* Over the last 5 years in particular, the Museum has been increasing Haida involvement in the interpretation, identification and exhibition of Haida material heritage.

Special Events During the Visit:

Tuesday Sept 8th: Welcome and Introduction to the Museum, 10 am – noon. Haida delegates will be officially welcomed to PRM. Collections and conservation staff and volunteers assisting with the visit will be introduced to Haida delegates, and a short orientation session will follow.

Wednesday Sept 9th: The Friends of the Museum will be hosting a dinner for the Haida at the Museum. There will be Friends and volunteers arriving at 5:00 p.m. to set up for the dinner.

Thursday Sept 10th: Haida Film Night. There will be a screening of the documentary, *Stolen Spirits of Haida Gwaii*, at the Pauling Centre on Banbury Road, followed by a Q&A period with Haidas, and refreshments. Doors open at 7 pm. If you wish to attend, please contact Laura Peers to ensure seat availability.

Sunday Sept 13th: A Haida Happening, Oxford Open Doors, 1-4 pm, at the Museum. This is a family-orientated, free, afternoon event. The Haidas will be dancing and singing, demonstrating weaving techniques, speaking with visitors in the Lower Gallery, and there will be puppet-making for families in the Temporary Exhibition Space.

Tuesday Sept 15th: Farewell Dinner for all PRM Staff and Haidas. This will be a catered dinner at the museum from 5 pm. Please Save the Date!!

Wednesday Sept 16th: Conference for UK Curators and Haidas. Curatorial staff from across the UK will be travelling to Oxford to meet Haidas and introduce their Haida/Northwest Coast collections to them. 10 am – 3pm, Lecture Theatre.

Wednesday Sept 16th: Haidas depart for London and the British Museum, 4 pm.

Courtesy, Pitt Rivers Museum, University of Oxford

Bibliography

Adams, Geraldine Kendal. 2018. 'Macron report advocates permanent return of colonial-era African objects'. *Museums Association News*, 28 November 2018. Accessed online at www.museumsassociation.org/museums-journal/news/28112018-macron-report-repatriation

Biggar, Nigel. 2020. 'Let's stop this descent into self-pitying Empire shame over our universities' ancient artefacts'. *The Telegraph*, 10 February 2020. Accessed online at www.telegraph.co.uk/news/2020/02/10/stop-descent-self-pitying-empire-shame-universities-ancient/

Brown, Mark. 2016. 'One in five regional museums at least part closed in 2015, says report'. *The Guardian*, 13 January 2016. Accessed online at www.theguardian.com/culture/2016/jan/13/one-in-five-regional-museums-at-least-part-closed-in-2015-says-report

Brown, Mark. 2019. 'British Museum chief – taking the Parthenon marbles was creative'. *The Guardian*, 28 January 2019. Accessed online at www.theguardian.com/artanddesign/2019/jan/28/british-museum-chief-taking-the-parthenon-marbles-was-creative

Clerici, Nadia. 2002. 'Indian voices in the European context' in *European Review of Native American Studies*, Vol. 16, Issue. 2, pp.1–10

Clifford, James. 1999 [1997]. 'Museums as contact zones' in *Representing the Nation: A Reader*, ed. David Boswell & Jessica Evans. London & New York: Routledge, pp.435–57

Collison, Nika. 2016. 'An unbroken line: Haida art and culture'. Paper presented at the Canada Seminar, University of Oxford, Oxford, 12 February 2016

Collison, Jisgang Nika & Nicola Levell. 2018. 'Curators talk: A conversation' in *BC Studies*, No. 199: Indigeneities and Museums: Ongoing Conversations – Autumn 2018

Collison, Jisgang Nika, Sdaahl K'awaas Lucy Bell & Lou-ann Neel. 2019. *Indigenous Repatriation Handbook*. Royal BC Museum, Victoria

Cooper, Jago. 2020. 'The Arctic experience of climate change'. *British Museum Blog*, 20 November 2020. Accessed online at https://blog.britishmuseum.org/the-arctic-experience-of-climate-change/

Davy, Jack. 2021. *Miniaturisation on the Northwest Coast: To Leave It for Memory*. University of British Columbia Press, Vancouver (forthcoming)

Edwards, Elizabeth, 2018. 'Addressing colonial narratives in museums'. *The British Academy Blog*, 19 April 2018. Accessed online at www.thebritishacademy.ac.uk/blog/addressing-colonial-narratives-museums/

Friedman, Vanessa. 2019. 'Dior finally says no to sauvage'. *New York Times*, 13 September 2019. Accessed online at www.nytimes.com/2019/09/13/style/dior-sauvage-cultural-appropriation.html

Glass, Aaron. 1999. 'Review: *Aboriginal Slavery on the Northwest Coast of North America* by Leland Donald' in *American Indian Quarterly*, Vol. 23, No. 3/4 (Summer-Autumn, 1999), pp.191–3

Hatfield, Boodle. 2019. 'UK won't repatriate looted artefacts, says UK culture secretary'. *Lexology.com*. Accessed online at www.lexology.com/library/detail.aspx?g=dc0c2615-2287-4403-b5f2-9ca5276dfb93

Heal, Sharon. 2019. 'Restitution: A blunt 'no' is not enough'. *Museums Association News*, 23 April 2019. Accessed online at www.museumsassociation.org/comment/23042019-restitution-a-blunt-no-is-not-enough

Hickley, Catherine. 2019i. 'Dutch museums take initiative to repatriate colonial-era artefacts'. *The Art Newspaper*, 14 March 2019. Accessed online at www.theartnewspaper.com/news/dutch-museums-take-initiative-to-repatriate-colonial-era-artefacts?fbclid=IwAR2xZAV_BWTnC2H8-FbsvUUHHYD5nm3FcwVQVv3x9Z5VLoyQilXfzRyf1Ho

Hickley, Catherine. 2019ii. 'Culture ministers from 16 German states agree to repatriate artefacts looted in colonial era'. *The Art Newspaper*, 14 March 2019. Accessed online at www.theartnewspaper.com/news/culture-ministers-from-16-german-states-agree-to-repatriate-artefacts-looted-in-colonial-era

Higgins, Charlotte. 2018. 'British Museum director Hartwig Fischer – there are no foreigners here – the museum is a world country'. *The Guardian*, 13 April 2018. Accessed online at www.theguardian.com/culture/2018/apr/13/british-museum-director-hartwig-fischer-there-are-no-foreigners-here-the-museum-is-a-world-country

Hochschild, Adam. 2020. 'The fight to decolonize the museum'. *The Atlantic*, January/February 2020. Accessed online at www.theatlantic.com/magazine/archive/2020/01/when-museums-have-ugly-pasts/603133/

Hunt, Tristram. 2019. 'Should museums return their colonial artefacts?' *The Guardian*, 29 June 2019. Accessed online at www.theguardian.com/culture/2019/jun/29/should-museums-return-their-colonial-artefacts

Janes, Robert. 2015. 'Prologue' in *We Are Coming Home: Repatriation and the Restoration of Blackfoot Cultural Confidence*. AU Press, Edmonton.

Jones, Jonathan. 2019. 'Let's not lose our marbles over the British Museum boss's remarks'. *The Guardian*, 29 January 2019. Accessed online at www.theguardian.com/artanddesign/2019/jan/29/british-museum-director-is-right-the-parthenon-marbles-belong-to-us-all

King, J. C. H. 2012. 'Art, ambiguity and the Haida Collection at the British Museum' in *American Indian Art Magazine*, Vol. 38, No.1, pp.56–65.

Livne, Inbal. 2020. 'Uncomfortable truths: Re-thinking the Powell Cotton story' in *Journal of Museum Ehtnography*, Vol. 33 (March 2020), pp.59–74.

Lundin, Emma. 2019. 'There is no longer any excuse for not repatriating museums' colonial art'. *Prospect Magazine*, 25 March 2019. Accessed online at www.prospectmagazine.co.uk/magazine/repatriation-museum-colonial-art-parthenon-marbles-easter-island

Mendoza, Neil. 2017. *The Mendoza Review: An independent review of museums in England*. Department for Digital, Culture, Media and Sport. London. Accessed online at https://assets.publishing.service.gov.uk/government/uploads/system/uploads/attachment_data/file/673935/The_Mendoza_Review_an_independent_review_of_museums_in_England.pdf

Museums Association. n.d. *Code of Ethics for Museums*, Museums Association, Accessed online at www.museumsassociation.org/download?id=1155827

Museums Association. 2019. *Empowering Collections Report*. Museums Association. Accessed online at www.museumsassociation.org/download?id=1262818

Noce, Vincent. 2018. 'Give Africa its art back' Macron's report says'. *The Art Newspaper*, 20 November 2018. Accessed online at www.theartnewspaper.com/news/give-africa-its-art-back-macron-s-report-says

Norman, Taylor, 2019i. *Bridging the divide: Reevaluating Native American displays in the British Museum and Horniman World Gallery*. Unpublished MA thesis, SOAS. Copy of document provided to author by Norman.

Norman, Taylor (@realtaynorman), 2019iii. Published on *Twitter*, 5 September 2019. Accessed online at https://twitter.com/realtaynorman/status/1169394131635884032

Northwest Territories Literacy Council. 2016. *hivulipita uqauhiit tuppaaqtauffaaqtut /awakening our ancestors' words*. Accessed online at www.mun.ca/isc2016/katingavik/hivulipta-uqauhiit-tuppaaqtauffaaqtut–awakening-our-ancestorsrsquo-words.html

Onciul, Bryony. 2015. *Museums, Heritage and Indigenous Voice: Decolonizing Engagement*. London & New York: Routledge

Orton, Amy. 2019. 'All of Leicester's museum curators are being made redundant'. *Leicester Mercury*, 7 April 2019. Accessed online at www.leicestermercury.co.uk/news/leicester-news/leicesters-museum-curators-being-made-2610639

Peers, Laura & Alison K. Brown (eds.). 2003. *Museums and Source Communities: A Routledge Reader*. London & New York: Routledge

Krmpotich, Cara & Laura Peers. 2013. *This Is Our Life: Haida Material Heritage and Changing Museum Practice*. Vancouver: University of British Columbia Press

Pomian, Krzysztof (trans. Elizabeth Wiles-Portier). 1990 [1987]. *Collectors and Curiosities: Paris and Venice, 1500–1800*. Cambridge: Polity Press

Postans, Adam. 2019. 'Two human skulls returned to Pacific island after decades on display in Bristol'. *Bristol Post*, 1 April 2019. Accessed online at www.bristolpost.co.uk/news/bristol-news/two-human-skulls-returned-remote-2707513

Procter, Alice. 2020. *The Whole Picture: The Colonial Story of the Art in Our Museums & Why We Need to Talk About It*. London: Cassell

Pratt, Mary Louise. 1991. 'Arts of the Contact Zone' in *Profession*, pp.33–40

Sarr, Felwine & Bénédicte Savoy. 2018. *The restitution of African cultural heritage: Toward a new relational ethics*. Ministère de la Culture, France. Paris. Accessed online at http://restitutionreport2018.com/sarr_savoy_en.pdf

Sanderson, David. 2019. 'Minister rules out return of treasures'. *The Times*, 22 April 2019. Accessed online at www.thetimes.co.uk/article/minister-rules-out-return-of-treasures-2jlf3qh63

Sayet, Madeline. 2019i. *Where We Belong*. Play performed at Globe Theatre, 17 June 2019. Copy of script provided to author by Sayet.

School of Advanced Research. 2019. 'Guidelines for Collaboration'. School of Advanced Research. Accessed online at https://guidelinesforcollaboration.info

Scott, Emmy (@EmmyNawjoopinga), 2019. Published on *Twitter*, 5 September 2019. Accessed online at https://twitter.com/EmmyNawjoopinga/status/1169621634896019461

Smithsonian Center for Folklife and Cultural Heritage. n.d. 'Shared stewardship of collections'. Smithsonian Center for Folklife and Cultural Heritage. Accessed online at https://folklife-media.si.edu/docs/folklife/Shared-Stewardship.pdf

Sodaro, Amy. 2018. *Exhibiting Atrocity: Memorial Museums and the Politics of Past Violence*. Camden: Rutgers University Press.

Steel, Patrick. 2013. Taylor: Croydon casting itself into cultural wilderness. *Museums Association News*. 9 November 2013. Accessed online at www.museumsassociation.org/news/19112013-taylor-croydon-casting-itself-into-cultural-wilderness

Sullivan, Nicola. 2015. DCMS budget cut will hit museums. *Museums Association News*. 9 June 2015. Accessed online at www.museumsassociation.org/museums-journal/news/09062015-cost-cutting-measures-will-impact-museums

Interviews

Andersen, Chris. 2019. Interview with Jack Davy for *Beyond the Spectacle*, 26 September 2019

Baca, Danielle. 2019. Interview with Jack Davy for *Beyond the Spectacle*, 6 March 2019

Brave Rock, Eugene. 2018. Interview with Jack Davy for *Beyond the Spectacle*, 20 August 2018

Burke, Kimonee. 2019. Interview with Jack Davy for *Beyond the Spectacle*, 23 September 2019

Coombes, Linda. 2019. Interview with Jack Davy for *Beyond the Spectacle*, 11 April 2019

Hastings Museum staff (including Damian Etherington & Eleanor Lanyon). 2019. Interview with Jack Davy for *Beyond the Spectacle*, 2 September 2019

Marlowe, Jenny. 2020. Interview with Jack Davy for *Beyond the Spectacle*, 6 & 15 May 2020

Norman, Taylor. 2019ii. Interview with Jack Davy for *Beyond the Spectacle*, 17 May 2019

Peters, Paula, 2019. Interview with Jack Davy for *Beyond the Spectacle*, 11 April 2019

Sayet, Madeline. 2019ii. Interview with Jack Davy for *Beyond the Spectacle*, 19 June 2019

Sense, Sarah. 2019. Interview with Jack Davy for *Beyond the Spectacle*, 28 August 2019

Tasi Baker, Sierra. 2018. Interview with Jack Davy for Beyond the Spectacle, 18 August 2018

Acknowledgments

Many people played important roles in the development of this project. It emerged from and is part of the work of the Beyond the Spectacle project at the University of East Anglia and the University of Kent, funded by the Arts & Humanities Research Council and led by Prof. David Stirrup and Prof. Jacqueline Fear-Segal. Prof. Coll Thrush, project researcher Dr. Kate Rennard and administrator Dr. Charlie Hall provided key support. Supportive reads were provided by Prof. Laura Peers and Catherine Haok.

The engagement and participation of Damian Etherington, Eleanor Lanyon and the team at Hastings Museum and Art Gallery was crucial, and their trailblazing on this subject speaks volumes to their professionalism. Special thanks are also due to Prof. Michael Rowlands and the team at Cambridge Elements for shepherding it through the publication process.

Most importantly, dedicated thanks are due to the Native North American scholars and artists who gave their time and expertise to this examination of their experiences in UK museum spaces. Prof. Chris Andersen, Danielle Baca, Eugene Brave Rock, Linda Coombes, Kimonee Burke, Jenny Marlowe, Taylor Norman, Paula Peters, Madeline Sayet, Sarah Sense, and Sierra Tasi Baker – this book is only possible thanks to your generosity and dedication, and I am very grateful.

Cambridge Elements ☰

Critical Heritage Studies

Kristian Kristiansen
University of Gothenburg

Michael Rowlands
UCL

Francis Nyamnjoh
University of Cape Town

Astrid Swenson
Bath University

Shu-Li Wang
Academia Sinica

Ola Wetterberg
University of Gothenburg

About the Series

This series focuses on the recently established field of Critical Heritage Studies. Interdisciplinary in character, it brings together contributions from experts working in a range of fields, including cultural management, anthropology, archaeology, politics, and law. The series will include volumes that demonstrate the impact of contemporary theoretical discourses on heritage found throughout the world, raising awareness of the acute relevance of critically analysing and understanding the way heritage is used today to form new futures.

Cambridge Elements ≡

Critical Heritage Studies

Elements in the Series

Printed in the United States
by Baker & Taylor Publisher Services